Senior
Spirituality

Senior Spirituality

Awakening Your Spiritual Potential

HAROLD R. NELSON

Harold R. Nelson

CHALICE PRESS

ST. LOUIS, MISSOURI

Biblical quotations, unless otherwise noted, are from the *New Revised Standard Version Bible,* copyright 1989, Division of Christian Education of the National Council of the Churches of Christ in the United States of America. Used by permission. All rights reserved.

Scripture quotations marked NKJV are taken from the *New King James Version.* Copyright © 1979, 1980, 1982 by Thomas Nelson, Inc. Used by permission. All rights reserved.

Cover art: © Digital Stock
Cover design: Elizabeth Wright
Interior design: Hui-chu Wang
Art direction: Elizabeth Wright

This book is printed on acid-free, recycled paper.

Visit Chalice Press on the World Wide Web at
www.chalicepress.com

10 9 8 7 6 5 4 3 2 1   04 05 06 07 08 09

Library of Congress Cataloging–in–Publication Data

Nelson, Harold R.
  Senior spirituality : awakening your spiritual potential / Harold R. Nelson.
    p. cm.
  ISBN 0-8272-3455-4 (pbk.)
  1. Aged–Religious life. 2. Spirituality. I. Title.
  BV4580.N45 2004
  248.8'5–dc22
                                                        2003026295

Printed in the United States of America

Contents

Acknowledgments

The creation of this book is by no means a solo effort. While I have conceived, imaged, and written the text, many persons have contributed their talents, in a variety of ways, to bring about the birthing of this book.

Following is a list of persons who have given generously of their time, energy, and talent, and I express my deep gratitude to each one:

Cynthia Carlson
Marjorie Finden
Leonard Holstad
Julie Ingle
Gisele Klemann
Evelyn Smith
Fritzi Lyon
Georgia Brauer
Arlene Carlson
Robert Hanson
Kenneth Ring

Additionally, I thank those residents of the La Posada Retirement Community who participated in the spirituality and loss and grief surveys.

In particular, I express my gratitude to Meg Park, my local editor and consultant, who made many insightful suggestions to make the book more readable and dynamic.

From the first day I began to write this book, my wife, Marguerite, has been an enthusiastic supporter of the project, and throughout the writing she has always been available for consultation and clarifying discussions. Her keen insights and practical suggestions have greatly enhanced the readability and quality of the book, and I am deeply grateful for her contribution.

Finally, I thank Dr. David Polk and the staff at Chalice Press for their excellent editorial work.

Harold R. Nelson
Green Valley, Arizona
November 20, 2003

Introduction

Oscar Anderson found it very difficult to eke out a living on his Kansas farm in the dust bowl days of the 1930s. In the arid conditions of those days, with little—if any—rainfall, Oscar had many crop failures. Somehow his growing family got by, but barely.

What Oscar did not know is that black gold was buried on his farm. Had he known that, and been able to tap it, his economic woes would have been over! In the early 1950s several productive oil wells were discovered on the land where Oscar used to farm.

I see a parallel between Oscar's buried black gold and dormant spirituality. Though every person is endowed with it, spirituality may lie buried and untapped, leaving that person in spiritual poverty.

This book is about the awakening of spirituality so that it may become a fountain of life, health, strength, and courage. If the fountain of spirituality is kept open and unrestricted, it will turn out to be a wellspring of joy, peace, and love, blessing you all the days of your life.

This book is addressed to seniors who want to learn about and develop their own spirituality. However, it may also be useful for those who are thinking about when they will be seniors.

The journey of spirituality may be divided into three stages: the apprentice, the disciple, and the master. The apprentice looks to a disciple or a master to teach him or her the way and skills of spirituality. The disciple is one who is firmly committed to follow the spiritual path, has gained many skills and insights, and who enthusiastically shares his or her growing spirituality with others.

The marks of a master are humility, contentment, wisdom, and a vast knowledge of the ways of spirituality. A master is one who has an intimate relationship with the "Master of Masters" and reflects a radiant spirit. To be in the presence of a master is in itself a learning experience. Yes, there are masters walking among us today. They will not tell you so, but you will feel their presence.

Spirituality covers such a vast territory that no one, not even a master, ever stops learning.

This book is a spiritual road map, which will guide you over a human-divine landscape. Each chapter will introduce you to a new, but perhaps also familiar, territory. As I have written the seven chapters of this book, I have had a learning and growing experience. I hope that you, while reading this book, may also find it to be a learning and growing experience.

Chapter 1, "Discovering Spirituality," explores the source of spirituality, its manifestations, and such topics as guidance, wellness, and being in-spirited. Classic ways of awakening spirituality, such as quests and journeys, are examined in *The Pilgrim's Progress* and *The Legend of the Holy Grail.* Taking one's own spiritual journey and looking at one's own human-divine experience over a lifetime also helps one to discover the way of the Spirit. The importance of establishing one's own inner listening post is discussed in the final pages of this chapter.

Chapter 2 points out that many of us learn best through the example of a model. This chapter presents five diverse models. They are not perfect, nor are they to be copied. Rather, they are intended to give us courage in the face of great difficulties and encourage and inspire us to reach for greater heights of spirituality.

In chapter 3 the many and difficult adversities encountered on the journey of life are considered. Illness and hospitalization are viewed in the context of the rites of passage. Diseases such as chronic diabetes, multiple sclerosis, and Alzheimer's are shown from the perspective of persons and families experiencing them. The dynamics of pain, its effects, and control of pain are discussed.

In this chapter, suffering is viewed as a redemptive experience out of which may flow purification, insights, and character building. Dread and despair may also be turned into hope. The final section of this chapter considers the physical, emotional, and mental aspects of stress and how it may be managed. To determine how much stress you have accumulated, a life event change scale is included.

Chapter 4 discusses the power of imagination to create out of nothingness, and the human capacity to be co-creators with God. A history of the use of imagination as healer is explored in Shamanism, the Temples of Asciepius, and Christian healing.

In contemporary times, mind-body medicine, through study, research, and case presentations, has emerged as an effective healer. The power of suggestion, spontaneous healing, and the immune system are areas in which mind-body medicine has made much progress. Interesting case examples demonstrate that some unusual healings have occurred. Lawrence Le Shan's *Consciousness, Healing and Research Project* notes that an altered state of consciousness is the means used by many healers to bring about healing.

In the last part of this chapter, ten healing modalities are discussed, including contemplation, guided imagery, and therapeutic touch.

The main focus of chapter 5 is on dealing with grief and loss. The importance of giving a full expression to loss is what grief work is about. Various categories of loss are identified and discussed. Four essential tasks of grief are noted. A listing of the physical and feeling sensations of grief serves to let the griever know he or she is on track.

Chapter 6 stresses the importance of being prepared for death and laments the fact that so many seem unprepared. Attention is called to the many reminders that death is coming, such as the deaths of loved ones and friends, illnesses, brushes with death, wakes, funerals, memorial services, and cemeteries.

Preparation for death involves making specific plans in the here and now. Such plans can be made by looking at death in the context of three stages: the pre-death stage, the death stage (the death moment), and the after-death stage. Preparing well for each stage is the key to dying well. The completion of unfinished relational business is paramount for a peaceful death. Music therapy may also be very soothing at the moment of death.

What do you believe about afterlife? What do we know about it? Chapter 7 considers the evidence as told by one who experienced it, an eyewitness. In this chapter, the experienced one and the eyewitness tell the story in their own words. Though many evidences for afterlife exist, this chapter will consider only eight. These evidences are deathbed visions, near-death experience (NDE), after-death communication (ADC), immortality, resurrection, poetry, mysticism, and separation of body and spirit.

In order that the reader might become familiar with what I mean by spirituality, I offer the following reflections.

Spirituality is the opposite of materiality. While the material world is visible, dense, and measurable, the spiritual world is invisible, weightless, and immeasurable. In the world of materiality, time, space, and senses are foundational stones of reality; but in the world of spirituality, senses, time, and space cease to exist. In the material realm the senses (touch, taste, smell, sight, and hearing) are used to understand the universe, but in the spiritual realm the sensory reality is transcended and an inner spirit, sometimes referred to as heart or soul, gives understanding, guidance, and direction.

Spirituality is like the wind, and although it cannot be seen, it is nevertheless felt. Spirituality is felt when love, joy, and peace are expressed between human beings. Spirituality is also the energy and power that undergird life. When a person's body dies, it is commonly understood that the spirit, or animating life energy, has left the body. Spirituality energizes all living things; it is the twinkle in the eyes and the glow or radiance that lights up a personality.

Spirituality is connectedness. It is a feeling of being connected and in relationship with God, neighbor, self, and creation. It is a feeling of oneness with the plant and animal kingdoms. Spirituality is living in harmony with all of creation and appreciating its beauty and diversity.

Spirituality is not the same as religion. Organized religion may deal with externals such as creeds, doctrines, rituals, and attendance at worship services, but spirituality is an internal seeking and realization of God at a personal level. It is a definite plus when organized religion feeds into and enhances spirituality.

Spirituality is the grateful response of the soul to a loving and merciful God whose presence fills the universe and has bestowed on humankind the gift of life. Spirituality is indestructible. It is the "divine spark" within, which has no end. Words cannot describe the true essence of spirituality. The mystery of spirituality is well captured in the words of Albert Einstein:

> The most beautiful thing we can experience is the mysterious. It is the source of all true Art and Science. He to whom this emotion is a stranger, who can no longer pause to wonder and stand rapt in awe, is as good as dead; his eyes are closed.[1]

CHAPTER 1

Discovering Spirituality

If it is true that each person is endowed with an animating spirit, where can it be found? It is easy to see that each person is endowed with a body because we can see, touch, and feel it. Unlike the body, the spirit cannot be seen or touched. If spirit cannot be known through a sensory approach, how then may it be discovered?

Perhaps an analogy may help. Spirit may be compared to wind (Jn. 3:8). Although we do not see wind as a substance, we readily feel its affects. We see it in the waving of tree branches, feel the force of it on our faces, or behold its awesome power in a hurricane or tornado. The effects of spirit may likewise be felt in a person who has a radiant countenance; energy and enthusiasm for living; and peace, love, and tranquility. The effects of spirit may also be observed in a person who has a meaning to live for, and a mission to fulfill.

Are there such people? To be sure! Such people walk among us each day, though they do not parade their piety. My mother was such a person. Though far from perfect, she bore the marks of an animating spirit in her life.

Inspiration

To further delve into the discovery of spirit, let us take a look at the word *inspiration*. We commonly use this word in everyday talk: "Wasn't that an inspiring performance?" "She is an inspiring person," and "I felt inspired by that speech."

To be inspired is to be "in-spirited." It is to "breathe in spirit" and to become animated with life. It can be quickly grasped that spirit is the mother of life. The stark realization of this truth comes at death, when the spirit departs from the body. Once the spirit departs, only a corpse remains.

If a person can be "inspirited," so can a person be "dispirited," which is what we mean when we say "her spirit is broken" or "his spirit fell." When people are dispirited, they have a low level of spirit; and when inspirited, they have a high level of spirit. In order to gain a more graphic picture of spirit level, let us assume it can be measured and give it a range of 0–100. This may also be called a "spirit-titre level," as Sydney Jourard calls it in his book *The Transparent Self*.[1] People who are highly inspirited may have a spirit titre of 70–100, those moderately inspirited 30–70, and those who are dispirited a range of 0–30.

It might be appropriate now to ask a pertinent question: What is the relationship between spirit titre and wellness? What keeps one person well in dire and difficult circumstances while another gives up and falls ill? What kept Victor Frankl going in the harsh and brutal circumstances of a Nazi concentration camp while many of his comrades gave up hope, became depressed, and died?[2] Could it be because Frankl maintained a high spirit titre? What kept his spirit so buoyed? One reason was that he had pieces of an unpublished manuscript hidden that needed to be published at some future time. This fact was the strong meaning and motivation that kept him well enough to survive the severe deprivations of a concentration camp.

It is well established today in mind-body studies that wellness and a healthy immune system rest on the degree of hope, love, peace, truth, and faith one builds life upon.[3]

If one considers one's own spirit titre level (and it is bound to fluctuate), cannot one gain a clue as to the presence of an indwelling spirit? I recognize that some days I am more receptive to spirit than on other days. Thus, on days I am dispirited, I welcome less spirit into my life; and on days when I am highly inspirited, I obviously have chosen a fullness of the spirit. The choice of whether to be dispirited or inspirited is up to each one of us. The spirit is always available, and we need but welcome it into our lives. The key to choosing inspiration is to be aware that there is a choice. For example, do I choose to forgive a person who has wronged or hurt me? If I choose to forgive, then peace and love will flow through my heart; but if I am unforgiving, bitterness and resentment will close down my heart. Choosing to forgive will help maintain a high spirit titre, while choosing not to forgive will lower spirit titre.

A good question to ask each day is, How is my spirit titre level? If dispirited, what choices can be made to move to a level of inspiration?

Once we have discovered the presence of an indwelling spirit, the question arises: Is our spirit connected to a larger spirit force, a universal spirit? My answer is a resounding yes! Indeed, the very source of our indwelling spirit is Universal Spirit, or God. The Spirit of God pervades the entire universe. God's spirit is present everywhere and has placed a divine spark, a divine image, and a "spirit center" in each person. Therefore, when you discover indwelling spirit, you also discover Universal Spirit.

Ways to Discover Spirituality

How else may spirituality be discovered? One may undertake a quest for spirituality. There is a rich history in literature, poetry, and legend about those who have journeyed over dangerous turf to find the pearl of great price. What is this pearl of great price for which many have risked life and limb? It is the inner pearl of divine nature, the spirit center by which anything in the temporal world pales in comparison.

Why do we set out on a quest for spirituality? Is it to satisfy the inner yearning of the heart? Even if we have acquired a beautiful home, the best automobiles, status, reputation, fame, and the financial means to live comfortably in retirement, we may one day discover a restlessness, an inner gnawing that says something is missing. From where does the feeling come that something is missing? Could it be the voice of our indwelling spirit yearning to be satisfied? Perhaps this spiritual voice had been muffled or silenced earlier, but now, in the fall season of life, it wants to be heard and satisfied. Augustine put it very aptly when he declared, "We are restless, O Lord, until we find our rest in Thee."[4]

Pay careful attention to your inward yearnings and longings, for they could lead you to discover spiritual well-being and a life of fullness. Don't expect your spiritual journey to be easy. The journey will require patience, discipline, perseverance, and risk taking.

One of the classic stories of spiritual journey is John Bunyan's *The Pilgrim's Progress.*[5] Starting out from the city of destruction, Christian is compelled to make a journey into unknown and perilous territory, even if it means leaving family behind. He gets bogged down in the "Slough of Despond," is distracted by false guides, faces lions and a giant, climbs the hill of difficulty, and at last arrives at the gate to the celestial city. Here, he basks in the radiance and light of the heavenly realm, his spirit finding fulfillment, peace, and rest. On the journey he often feels bewildered, frightened, and ready to give up, but at each time of discouragement, a guide or helper appears to bring understanding, encouragement, and direction.

Christian's arduous journey to the celestial city has important lessons to teach us: (1) We need to pay attention to inner longings of the spirit;

(2) we must have a willingness to set out on a journey into unknown territory; (3) we must be willing to make the journey alone; (4) we need to persevere, even when faced with great difficulties; (5) we do well to accept the counsel of guides along the way who provide us with understanding and direction; and (6) it is necessary to keep the goal of our journey in clear focus. John Bunyan's *The Pilgrim's Progress,* written three and one-half centuries ago, is amazingly relevant for the spiritual traveler of today.

Let us take a look at another spiritual quest using the legend of the Holy Grail.[6] According to the legend, which took shape in the twelfth and thirteenth centuries in Europe, the Holy Grail is the chalice used at the Last Supper. It is kept in a castle in which the wounded fisher king lives. The fisher king moans about his painful wound and does not know how to receive the help of this Holy Grail, but the court fool tells him that one day an innocent fool will appear to help. The innocent fool is Parsifal, and he is naive, untutored, and fatherless, clad in homespun clothes.

One day Parsifal sees five knights ride by, and he is so dazzled that he can think of nothing else but becoming a knight. His mother, Heart Sorrow, is afraid to let him go, but it is useless for her to protest. He meets a red knight and asks how he may be knighted. The red knight laughs at Parsifal, but sends him on to King Arthur's Court. Somehow, the naive lad in homespun clothes gains an audience with King Arthur, and while the two talk, a fair damsel begins to laugh. She hasn't laughed in six years, and it has been said that whoever could make her laugh is mightier than the best of knights. King Arthur is impressed and knights Parsifal on the spot.

Parsifal wants the armor of the red knight and is told by King Arthur that he can have it if he can get it. Parsifal finds the red knight and, with a sword given to him by his page, slays the knight. Parsifal, now properly equipped and having been given instructions along the way, sets out in search of the Holy Grail. When he arrives at the castle where the Holy Grail is kept, there is an important question he must ask. On his first appearance he forgets, but the second time he remembers. The question is, "Whom does the Grail serve?" The answer comes back: "The Grail serves the Grail King." At this moment the wounded fisher king is healed, and the entire kingdom, which has been desolate, comes alive.

What does the Holy Grail legend teach those of us who are on a quest for spirituality? The major teaching of the legend is that a proper understanding of the Holy Grail is fundamental. The Holy Grail serves the Grail King–God. The focal point is adoration, worship, and service to God. Once we see that the Holy Grail points to God, and that this God is both the beginning and ending of our mysterious and arduous journey, all else falls into place. As the wounded fisher king was healed, so will we be healed. If one seeks the Holy Grail to find happiness, one is missing the mark. Happiness is a byproduct of serving the Grail King (God). The truth of this has been borne out over and over again in my daily experience. My greatest happiness is found as I serve others, not as I serve myself. The quest of spirituality is not happiness or comfort, but it is to know and serve God.

What about the journey to reach the Holy Grail? This is where Parsifal may become our teacher. Parsifal shows us that there is power in the childhood innocence that leads to humility. What is humility? It is approaching life and all its problems without pretense, without deceit, but innocently, honestly, and directly. Like Parsifal, we must be willing to ask questions (though some may seem foolish) and receive instructions. If we can provoke laughter along the way, especially in those who have not laughed in years, we will be twice blessed. I have always been blessed when helping an overly serious soul to laugh. Laughter lightens the heavy load and creates a sense of well-being.

Parsifal reached the castle through the power of humility. We can also fulfill our spiritual destiny through the power of humility. Humility opens doors and conquers obstacles, but arrogance and pride close doors.

There remains one more important lesson to draw from the Holy Grail legend. Spiritual growth and maturation may occur while retaining innocence and humility. Parsifal was far wiser at the end of his arduous journey than at the beginning. The maturation was the result of asking questions, receiving instructions, facing challenges, and keeping focused on the goals of knighthood and finding the Holy Grail.

It is easy to become conceited and feel wiser than others who have learned less (in our judgment) than we have on the spiritual path. When we perceive maturation has occurred, it is a cause for inner rejoicing, but never to feel superior over anyone else. Is it not true that the great people in life are the truly humble? They retain the innocence of the child, are often caught up in wonder and awe, and never stop learning and growing.

Imagine a Golden Windmill

What might a quest for spirituality look like today? Is there a legend or a myth that could be meaningful? We need only to use our imagination. Let us suppose there is a golden windmill in the midst of a desert oasis. What is so attractive and appealing about a golden windmill? The legend that has sprung up is that to drink from its pure waters, one will gain spiritual illumination. Furthermore, one will understand the mysteries of life and death and behold the presence of God face-to-face. Moreover, the golden windmill and oasis will be a place of sublime peace and rest. It is by no means an easy task to find the golden windmill set in the midst of a beautiful oasis. Many mirages may appear to distract the desert traveler.

What are mirages? Mirages are fleeting images that promise a golden windmill, but as one travels toward them, they turn out to be nothing at all. The desert traveler pursuing a mirage only ends up frustrated, confused, anxious, and full of despair. Over the centuries, alluring and distracting mirages haven't changed much, although they may be dressed differently. There is still the mirage of greed. If I only had this or that, my life could be better. But the mirage of greed, far from producing a golden windmill in the end, results in nothingness and emptiness. Other mirages beckoning the desert traveler are pride (egocentricity), lust (desires of flesh), status, fame, power, and superiority. What all these mirages have in common is that they fail to satisfy the deepest longings and yearnings of indwelling spirit.

What path will lead the weary desert traveler to the golden windmill? If we walk the path of truth, kindness, compassion, gentleness, gratitude, peace, discipline, and—above all—love, one day we will reach the golden windmill set in the midst of a beautiful oasis. Because we human beings are prone to error, it is likely that we will be lured by several distracting mirages. In my own journey I have been distracted many times, only to come away unfilled.

I have always believed that discovering the fullness of our spirituality is a participatory event. So it is that when we reach the oasis and the golden windmill, we need to release the lever that will allow the windmill to start pumping the pure water of spiritual illumination.

I grew up in a farming community in Kansas, and the windmill was a necessary fixture on most farms. I recall how pleasant it was on a hot summer day to release the lever on the windmill, pick up the tin cup hanging on a hook, and enjoy a fresh, cool drink of well water. If I had sat by the windmill wishing for a drink of water, nothing would have happened.

The point I am making is that the awakening of our spiritual nature is not simply God as initiator and a human being as passive object, but it is a process in which both participate. While it is true that God provides illumination, human beings must release the lever, allowing it to happen.

The golden windmill and the beautiful desert oasis are the creation of my own imagination. The spiritual realities to which they point, such as the presence of God, illumination, and sublime peace and rest, are really what count.

My Personal Journey

The discovery of spirituality may be told through legends, symbols, and journeys of the soul. I would like, at this point, to share my own spiritual journey.

As far back as I can remember I have had a yearning for God. I wanted to be closer to God, to be known by God, and to know God for myself. Through Bible stories told by pastors, teachers, and my mother, I learned about God's dealings with humankind, God's long-suffering love, and God's incarnation in Jesus Christ of Nazareth. All these stories increased my yearnings and longings for God. I strongly identified with the fourth beatitude of Jesus, which declares, "Blessed are those who hunger and thirst for righteousness, for they will be filled" (Mt. 5:6). For "righteousness," I often substituted "God." I had plenty of hunger and thirst for God, and I still do. Perhaps I always will, as long as I am dwelling on this earthly plane. I feel good about this, for I know it is God who has put such yearnings inside of me. The promise of the fourth beatitude for satisfaction has come through to me in a feeling of belonging. Yes, I really do belong to God. I am one of God's children. To me, the yearnings and satisfactions have always gone together. They are inseparable.

My spiritual journey is made up of outward and inward components. The former consists of input through lectures, reading, study, stories, dialogue, worship services, caring for others, poetry, personal journaling, and writing. The outward spiritual journey is an outgrowth of the inward component. Yet the outward component alone will never satisfy the deep yearnings of the heart. I responded to my heartfelt yearnings early by deciding to be a disciple of Jesus Christ. This decision was made early in life, at about eleven years of age. My teenage and young adult years were times of exploration, curiosity, questioning, doubting, and seeking an identity. A year spent in the U.S. Navy during the close of World War II greatly expanded the perceptions of my life and world. As I entered Kansas State University in the fall of 1946, I was unsure of my vocational calling. What was I to do with my life? At first, I thought I would be a mechanical engineer. After one semester I found out I was not suited for that profession. I moved on into the field of geology, but I was still restless and uncertain of my calling. Slowly it began to dawn on me that I was best suited to work with people in a helping profession. Acting on this intuitive hunch, I took the necessary courses to qualify for a teacher's certificate. After teaching high school for one year, a deeper yearning and calling seemed to be taking hold of me. I would serve God and people by becoming a pastor. This prospect excited me, so I made plans to attend seminary. My theological education was challenging and opened up new doors of understanding and inquiry. After graduating from North Park Theological Seminary in Chicago, I served as pastor to three different congregations. I found that I enjoyed working with people and serving as a spiritual counselor and teacher.

Unexpectedly, in the summer of 1958 a call came, followed by a letter inviting me to become a hospital chaplain and supervisor of clinical pastoral education. In this capacity, I would minister to hospitalized patients and supervise pastors and seminary students of all faiths in the art of pastoral care. I was excited about this new twist in my spiritual journey, for it would involve further schooling and learning for me.

To some extent in seminary studies, and to a larger extent in postgraduate studies at Garrett-Northwestern University, the inward aspect of my spirituality began to develop. I was intrigued when reading about the "mystics" of the church, for they spoke of what was happening on the inside. They had formed an intimate relationship with the Divine Presence. I am referring here to such mystics as St. John of the Cross, St. Theresa of Avila, Meister Eckhart, and others.

Being a hospital chaplain in an acute medical center on Chicago's north side gave me ample opportunity to continue my discovery of spirituality. The patient became my teacher. I learned from the patient what it was like to face severe physical limitations, terminal illness, dying, death, loss, and grief. I found that it was connectedness to God or to a higher power that kept many going. Prayer was the connecting point.

Because I was intrigued with the question of how patients made use of spirituality to face illness, I did a master's thesis in 1961 on "The Religious Responses of a Group of Surgically Treated Cancer and Suspected Cancer Patients." The study showed that patients who had developed a spiritual philosophy demonstrated an attitude of acceptance, formed deeper relationships with the chaplain and hospital staff, and felt a connection with God. The findings of this study taught me that spirituality was real at the battlefronts of life.

Patients, their families, and clinical pastoral education students presented me with a unique opportunity to study spirituality firsthand. I would ask questions such as "How was God present during your critical incident?" and "What kept you going?" As I assisted others in discovering the movement of the spirit in their lives, I was also discovering the workings of spirit in my own life. I found that spiritual revelations flowed best out of a relationship of mutuality and trust.

During forty years of active pastoral ministry, my learning has taken place in a crucible of human suffering, including my own. I have walked through the dark night of the soul and ascended to the mount of spiritual inspiration. I have discovered and awakened my own spirituality to a greater degree than when I first began. I am still in process. The yearning for God continues. It was no accident that I became a hospital chaplain and teacher and supervisor in the art of pastoral care. I needed to be in pastoral ministry to learn the ways the spirit works in my life as well as in the lives of others. Regardless of one's profession, trade, or occupation, if we listen, spiritual insights and lessons will be learned.

Awakened by the Crisis of Illness

The crisis of illness can and often does awaken spirituality. When we have exhausted all options in the hope of keeping the physical body going, where does one turn for help?

A very striking illustration of how the crisis of illness may awaken spirituality appeared in the May 1999 issue of *The Readers Digest.* Mary Catherine Fish authored it in the condensed article "Letting Go." In this article she gave a very personalized and touching account of her husband Tom's diagnosis with a fast-growing malignant brain tumor, the difficult surgeries, and treatments of radiation and chemotherapy. When Mary realized the odds for Tom's survival were small, she reached out for spiritual help. Not knowing how to pray, but wishing to do so, she consulted her Aunt Marcella, who suggested that the prayer was already in her heart. This brought a sense of relief to Mary. While holding her husband's hand, she prayed her first prayer, which touched me deeply. It went like this:

> I am scared. Help me to keep my heart open. Show us what to do. You know how much Tom and I love each other. Keep us here together and help us. We will face what situations we must, but we want to go on with our life together. We will face this, but please help us. Amen.[7]

Through the crisis of a serious and life-threatening illness, Mary and Tom's dormant spirituality was awakened. Once the door of spirituality was opened, the strength to face dying, death, and living life to the fullest came to both Mary and Tom. When Tom died early on a summer morning, Mary was with him as he drew his last breath. The extent of Mary's spiritual growth may be felt in her words, uttered as she stood by Tom's dead body.

> I envisioned Tom's spirit as light moving toward an even larger light. I felt something I had never felt before, a sense of mystery. I sensed Tom had been lifted up and I was in awe. I have also learned that love endures beyond pain and sorrow. It is the one thing that outlasts all.[8]

Mary's development of a spiritual perspective enabled her to go through the painful ordeal of Tom's dying and death and the dark days of loss and grief. In my experience as a hospital chaplain, her story is a familiar one. Is it possible that the crisis of illness is a blessing in disguise? This has surely been the case with me. Each crisis of illness or physical limitation I have faced has deepened my spirituality and given me strength to go forward.

The Still Small Voice

Amid the clamor of many voices trying to gain your attention in this multimedia age, have you taken the time to listen to the "still small voice" that resides in the depths of your soul? If you have, you are finding another way to discover your spirituality. If you are intent about listening for and hearing the voice of God, it will require closing down the multitude of voices both outside and inside of you that claim your attention.

An illustration will make clear the point I wish to get across. The prophet Elijah had just won a great victory over the false prophets of Baal. However, this victory, in which all the prophets of Baal had been destroyed, greatly angered Queen Jezebel. She sent Elijah a message saying she would have him killed within one day's time. Upon hearing this news, Elijah fled for the wilderness (1 Kings 19:1–11). All alone in the wilderness, he began to hear threatening inner voices. First he heard the voice of fear, then the voice of failure, and finally the voice of self-destruction. Can you identify with any of these negative voices? I can. From time to time during my lifespan I have heard all of these voices. I have struggled not to let any of these negative voices take over.

As Elijah moved into a cave on Mount Horeb, he heard the awesome voices of nature. First was the voice of a great wind, next the voice of a mighty earthquake, and finally the voice of a crackling fire. At this point Elijah was beginning to listen for the voice of God, but he perceived God was not present in any of the noisy displays of nature.

There are many noisy or spectacular voices that come our way, promising much but giving little, noises that end up leaving us empty. These are not voices of God. Even as Elijah did not find God in the noisy voices that came by him, neither are we likely to find God in the noisy voices of secular culture.

After all the noise had died down, Elijah heard the "still small voice" (1 Kings 19:12, NKJV). Elijah discovered the presence of God in stillness and quietness.

I am developing a listening post in which to discover the "still small voice." Early in the morning, before my day gets going, I sit quietly in my study waiting for the still small voice to make an impression on me. I'm listening not for an audible voice but for the awareness of divine presence. When there is a sense of peace, joy, and spiritual well-being, I am then aware of the still small voice. Such encounters are always upbuilding, positive, and encouraging. In sorting out all the voices we hear, remember that those that leave us with positive feelings come from the gentle, still small voice of God, while those that leave us feeling upset and anxious are usually negative voices of our own past conditioning. If we persist in the practice of stillness and quietness—the yearning to be in the divine presence—we will one day make it a reality.

I have noted only a few of the ways in which spirituality may be discovered. Since God is present everywhere, ways of discovering spirituality are unlimited. Some have discovered spirituality in the midst of close brushes with death, and others in the beauty and solitude of nature. When we are ready and open, spirituality will come to us in one way or another. The spiritual nature that has long been asleep will begin to grow, and if watered and nourished, it will one day flourish.

CHAPTER 2

Models of Spirituality

I have always learned best by seeing and experiencing a model in action. Most of the time, those models were unaware that I was picking up something important from them for my own life. My first models were my parents, teachers, and pastors, followed by baseball heroes and great American presidents such as Washington and Lincoln. Explorers such as Lewis and Clark, who blazed trails to open up the western territories, also inspired me. Models have influenced all of us.

Sometimes models lead us to a certain fork in the road, and then we cast about for a fresh model more pertinent to current needs. Occasionally, a model might lead us in the wrong direction, and once this awareness dawns, the model needs to be discarded.

The purpose of a model is to inspire us to develop our own lives to the fullest potential. Models are not to be copied as one would copy a blueprint. To do so would cause us to be unfaithful to our own unique destiny.

All human models are imperfect. In the long run, imperfection is a great blessing, for who can follow a perfect model? I can warm up to an imperfect model because such a model does not intimidate.

Who is a model of spirituality? In one way or another such a model points to a source greater than himself or herself. Spirituality models usually do not talk about that source; they are content to let the source work through their lives. In fact, they may be like the servants Jesus tells us about who seemed to be unaware they had cared for the sick, poor, and hungry (Mt. 25:34–40). These servants quietly did their good deeds without calling attention to themselves. So it is with many spirituality models. The source that flows through spirituality models is often identified as God, Jesus, the Holy Spirit, Higher Power, or The Light within.

I will present well-known and little-known models, all of whom have influenced my life in greater or lesser degrees. I have been taught and inspired by them all. I have not met these models, but they shine as bright stars bringing hope and courage to those who will listen.

Mother Teresa of Calcutta

The first model I will present is Mother Teresa. It is hard to think of a spirituality model who more completely personified the love of God in action than Mother Teresa. She chose to live and work among the poorest of the poor in the slums of Calcutta, India. Dedicating her life completely and totally to ministering to the dying poor, orphaned children, lepers, and all outcasts of humanity, she followed her own motto: "Love until it hurts."

Mother Teresa, named Agnes Bojaxhiu, was born in 1910, in Skopje, Albania. Raised in a devout Catholic home, she dreamed of becoming a nun and missionary. She found support from the local church and her mother, and accordingly joined The Order of Loretta Sisters of Ireland in September 1928.[1] In 1931, she became a teacher and later a principal in St. Mary's School in Calcutta. It was in September 1945, while riding in a train, that the call of God came to her to serve the "poorest of the poor." Although it meant saying goodbye to the Loretta Order, she soon embarked on a journey that would be the center of her attention and efforts for the rest of her life. By September 1948, Sister Teresa was on the streets of Calcutta caring for the dying, poor, and abandoned children. She had very little to give in the way of medicine and supplies, but she did have plenty of tender loving care.

In 1950, Mother Teresa founded the Missionaries of Charity. In August 1952, the first home for the dying and poor was opened in Calcutta, and in 1965, a home was set up outside India in Venezuela. By 1997, forty centers had been set up around the world.

How did all this growth take place? In 1969, Malcolm Muggeridge of BBC produced a film on the work of Mother Teresa, entitled *Something Beautiful for God*. Mother Teresa became world famous, and donations poured in to support her work from that time on. Ten years later (1979) she received the Nobel Peace Prize. Characteristically, she asked the organizers to cancel the celebration dinner with a request that the cost of the dinner be given to her work with the poorest of the poor.

It is hard to overestimate the profound influence Mother Teresa had on the lives of people of all faiths and walks of life. Muggeridge said that his meeting with Mother Teresa changed his whole life. "She has given me a new vision of what it means to be a Christian, of the amazing power of love, and how in one dedicated soul it can grow and spread to the whole world."

I will now sum up some of the qualities that made Mother Teresa such a dynamic spirituality model.

Humility was one of her outstanding qualities. Though she was acclaimed to be the most powerful woman in the world, she remained unimpressed by all the attention given her. Said Mother Teresa, "I am only a pencil in the hands of God."

A second quality was clear focus. She never lost sight of her mission to serve the poor. She did not hesitate to ask those in influential positions to help her meet a particular critical need for outcasts of society. For example, she asked the lieutenant governor in Calcutta for ten acres to build a clinic for lepers. He complied. Her focus was always on finding ways to meet the needs of the dying poor, abandoned children, lepers, and the disabled.

A third quality was giving compassionate, practical help. It was not enough to merely say kind words to the dying poor; what they needed was a bed, medicines, and nursing care. Mother Teresa rolled up her shirtsleeves and gave her care and skills to the poorest of the poor.

A fourth quality was identification with the poor. When she went to work among the poor, she put on a white cotton sari, like those worn by the poor women of India. She wore this uniform for the rest of her life. In all ways, Mother Teresa and the Missionaries of Charity strove to be like the poor. They knew that by identifying with the poor, their ministry would be more fruitful.

A fifth quality was selflessness and sacrifice. Mother Teresa put her own needs at the bottom of the scale, never asking anything for herself. Even when told to take it easy because of failing health in the early 1990s, she continued to be active. She once remarked that she would have plenty of time to rest in the hereafter. Mother Teresa was not driven by ego, but rather by compassion to minister to the dying, the poor, and the outcasts of society. On one occasion she said, "Being unwanted is the worst disease any human being can experience." By giving unselfishly of herself, Mother Teresa made many abandoned children feel wanted again.

One final quality was intimacy with God. Mother Teresa, as did all her Order, began each morning with one hour of prayer. She did not hesitate to pray for things she needed for her work. Her closeness to God can be readily seen in many of her statements. "I am a little pencil in the hand of God. He does the thinking. He does the writing. The pencil has only to be allowed to be used." The call to serve the poor was yet another instance of intimacy with God. In remembering her call, she said, "The message was very clear. I knew I had to devote myself to the poor by living among them. It was a command."[2]

Mother Teresa died on September 5, 1997. Dignitaries from around the world and common ordinary people came to pay their respects and say good-bye to a humble missionary who had given her last ounce of devotion to better the conditions of the poorest of the poor.

Martin Luther King, Jr.

My second spirituality model is Martin Luther King, Jr. He was born in Atlanta, Georgia, on January 15, 1929. His father was pastor of the Ebenezer Baptist Church, who disliked the unfair segregation laws that made the African American a second-class citizen. Thus, early in life, young Martin had a powerful role model in the person of his father, Martin Luther King, Sr.

Young Martin was a bright and eager learner. At age fifteen he entered Morehouse College in Atlanta.[3] What would he do with his life? He decided to be a minister, and in 1948 he enrolled at Crozer, a school of religion in Chester, Pennsylvania. He graduated three years later with an A average and was awarded $1,200. He decided to use this money to enroll at Boston University, where he met Coretta Scott. Martin's father married the two in June 1953 at the Ebenezer Baptist Church.

It was clear to King that African American people faced two major problems: segregation and poverty. King wanted to do something for his people, and it occurred to him that the nonviolent teaching of Gandhi might work. This teaching was also in accord with the teaching of Jesus, who said, "Love your enemies" (Mt. 5:44). King thought this would be the answer for African Americans in working to gain their civil rights.

King became pastor of the Dexter Avenue Baptist Church in Montgomery, Alabama, in 1954. From there he launched what became known as the civil rights movement. In 1955, after Rosa Parks was arrested for not giving up her seat on a bus, King called the African American community together, and they decided to boycott the Montgomery buses. King gave a speech that nonviolence must be practiced if the boycott was to be successful.

The boycott succeeded, but white racists didn't give up the fight. They arrested and jailed many African Americans, including King, threw bombs at homes, and made many threatening phone calls to King. King was charged with breaking a law that forbad boycotting and was ordered to stand trial in court. It was a dark time for King, and his spirits were at low ebb. He reached out to God in a prayer of anguish. "I'm at the end of my power. I have come to the place where I cannot face it alone." At that time, King sensed he was in the presence of God and heard an inner voice say, "Stand up for what is right, for what is true and I will be at your side forever."[4] This intimate encounter with the presence of God gave King the courage to continue the fight for civil rights. Victory came at last when the U.S. Supreme Court declared bus segregation to be unconstitutional. The victory at Montgomery showed that nonviolence would work. The African American community had not struck back at white racists but had sung freedom songs and had nonviolently resisted ill treatment.

King's fame spread, and he was hailed as a modern-day Moses. In May 1957, King spoke to a crowd of thirty-five thousand people gathered in Washington, D.C., and called for voter rights. By this time King's schedule had become so busy that he resigned from the Montgomery church and became his father's associate at Ebenezer Church in Atlanta in 1960. He scarcely had time to see his wife, Coretta, and his children. King had also been elected President of the Southern Christian Leadership Conference.

One of the most difficult times of the civil rights movement involved incidents in Birmingham, Alabama in 1963. Eugene "Bull" Connor, the police commissioner, was determined to put a stop to the civil rights marches. King was placed in jail, and then in solitary confinement, without bail. With the intervention of Attorney General Robert Kennedy, King was soon released from prison. Connor used clubs, police dogs, and fire hoses to repel African Americans. So many were arrested that the jails were filled.

In the end, most of the demands for equality in Birmingham were met, and a tremendous victory was won. It was a great victory for African Americans everywhere, and King was pleased, though he knew his work was far from over. In that same year, King addressed a quarter of a million people at the March on Washington with his "I Have a Dream" speech.

In October 1964, King won the Nobel Peace Prize. Coretta Scott King movingly describes the great celebration that took place in Oslo, Norway, in her book *My Life with Martin Luther King, Jr.*[5]

The march from Selma to Montgomery in 1965 was about winning voter rights for African American people. It was something King had been crusading for for several years. The Voting Rights Act of 1965 was a strong bill, and it was another impressive victory.

The end of earthly life came for King when he was shot and killed on the balcony of a Memphis motel on April 4, 1968. For King, death was not unexpected. He had often remarked that he could die at anytime. In his last speech, the night before he was killed, he said, "It [death] really doesn't matter with me now, because I've been to the mountaintop...and I've looked over and I've seen the Promised Land. I may not get there with you. But I want you to know tonight that we, as a people, will get to the Promised Land. And so I'm happy tonight. I'm not worried about anything; I'm not fearing any man. Mine eyes have seen the glory of the coming of the Lord."[6]

As a spirituality model, King has many inspirational qualities to offer. Consider the following:

- Vision: He looked ahead to a time when his people would be free and would dwell in equality with all peoples. This is most eloquently portrayed in his famous "I Have a Dream" speech.
- Faith: He believed, even in the darkest days, that the civil rights movement would ultimately prevail.
- Intimacy with God: King's close relationship with God brought peace in the midst of strife. It also was the source of empowerment.
- Perseverance: King endured beatings, jailing, bombings, stabbing, and verbal abuse. These adversities did not deter him from the main goal of winning civil rights for his people.
- Nonviolence: Peaceful marches and boycotts and not returning violence for violence were methods King successfully employed. He practiced the teaching of Jesus to "Love your enemies."
- Leadership: King led his people by example. He was in the forefront of peaceful demonstrations. His leadership also included careful planning, organization, and effective and inspirational public speaking.
- Empathy: King felt the hurts and abuses of African American people. He felt so deeply that he was willing to risk and sacrifice his own life.
- Compassion: King reached out with love to heal his people from years of abuse and maltreatment by white racists.
- Nonjudgmentalism: King did not judge those who opposed him. He regarded them as "white brothers."
- Humility: With all the fame and recognition that came his way, King did not let it go to his head. He remained humble and devoted to his cause.

Why did the U.S. Congress set aside a day in honor of Martin Luther King, Jr.? It was in recognition of the high ideals of freedom, truth, and justice for which he stood and gave his life. He has become a model for the American people, and for me he is an exceptional spirituality model.

Moses

My next spirituality model is Moses. The story of Moses' life, his qualities and characteristics, are recorded in the book of Exodus. Moses is an example of one who models humanity on the one hand and an intimate relationship with God on the other.

Moses was born at a time when the Pharaoh of Egypt had ordered all male Hebrew babies be put to death. Moses' mother, on seeing her beautiful son, devised a courageous plan to save Moses. She hid him for the first three months of his life, and then placed him in a basket among the reeds of the Nile River, posting his sister close by to see what would happen. The Pharaoh's daughter came down to bathe in the Nile, saw the basket, and sent one of her maids to fetch it. When the Pharaoh's daughter opened it and heard the Hebrew child crying, she took pity and decided to raise it as her son. Moses' own mother was appointed to nurse him.

Moses grew up and was educated in the courts of the king of Egypt. However, he never forgot his Hebrew heritage. One day, as he was observing the hard labors of his brethren, he noticed an Egyptian beating a Hebrew. After looking around and seeing no one watching, he struck the Egyptian down and buried him in the sand. The next day, however, as Moses was attempting to arbitrate a quarrel between two Hebrews, one of them revealed that he had seen Moses kill the Egyptian. This revelation struck great fear in Moses, for he realized the news would spread and his life would be in danger. Moses fled to Midian. There, he met the daughters of the local priest, who were about to draw water for their flocks. When Moses saw that some shepherds were driving off the daughters, he intervened and drove the shepherds away. When the daughters returned home and related the story, their father insisted that Moses be invited into their home. Moses settled in and soon married one of the daughters and became a shepherd (Exodus 2).

Moses as a young man had three strong characteristics. He was empathetic, feeling the heavy burdens that had been placed on his brethren by Egyptian taskmasters. Second, he let his anger get out of control, thus killing an Egyptian. His third characteristic was that he was a champion of the oppressed. As a young man, Moses was in the process of growth and development. He still had much to learn before he would one day become a trusted and respected leader of his people.

The next period in the life of Moses included encountering the Divine Presence and a call to responsibility. Moses was alone on Mount Horeb, finding pasture for the flocks of Jethro, his father-in-law, when he was attracted to a burning bush, which, though on fire, was not consumed. There, he heard the voice of God calling his name and telling him to remove his sandals, for he was standing on holy ground. God had heard the sufferings of the children of Israel and was committed to deliver them out of their oppression. But when God chose Moses to be leader of the venture, Moses stated several reasons why he could not assume this responsibility: Who was he to stand up to the Pharaoh? How would the Pharaoh ever believe him? Besides, he was slow of speech and tongue.

At last, when Moses ran out of excuses, God promised him that God would perform signs and miracles, and God appointed Moses' brother Aaron as a spokesperson. Moses then obeyed God's call to responsibility.[7]

Do you ever resist taking on a responsibility or task because you don't feel up to it, or you are convinced that you just don't have what it takes to get the job done? If so, then you can identify with Moses. How easy it is to forget that God has endowed us with the talent, power, and resources to take on the task before us.

Once Moses packed up, went to Egypt, took on the task of facing Pharaoh, and got involved in setting his people free, we heard no more excuses. Another step in the growth and development of Moses had taken place. It can also be noted that Moses was developing self-confidence, a characteristic so important that little can be accomplished without it. He was then able to stand up to and confront Pharaoh, as well as to address the elders of Israel. How did Moses develop self-confidence? Could it be that his growing relationship with God was the source? Moses was beginning to identify with a God of Being, with a God whose name was "I AM WHO I AM" (Ex. 3:14).

Learning to Be is the bottom line of self-confidence. Being is a state of grace allowing us to rest from work and to be fully content with who we are. The source of this grace is being connected to a God who exists in a state of pure being. When we come to dwell in this state of grace, we will experience a peace that passes all understanding and a deep sense that nothing, not even death itself, can disturb the state of being in which we have come to rest.

The next period in Moses' life was a forty-year sojourn in the wilderness. This was a most difficult and trying time, as he had to deal with the hostilities and rebelliousness of the children of Israel. At times, Moses gave way to impatience and anger, yet he still emerged as a strong and effective leader. One of the most striking developments of Moses, in this period, was his growing intimacy with God.[8] This period, often called the wilderness wanderings, brought to a close the life and work of the great servant Moses, who died at age 120, not having entered the promised land (Deut. 34:7).

Intimacy with God is a sought-after goal of anyone walking a spiritual path. There are three aspects to Moses' intimacy with God I will discuss here.

First of all is instrumentality. Moses was willing to be an instrument in the hand of God for the accomplishment of God's purposes. Consider that Moses was God's spokesperson to Pharaoh and that the staff he carried to perform such miracles as the parting of the Red Sea was just another way that God worked through Moses. Moses was also the instrument by which the Ten Commandments were delivered to the children of Israel. The word *channel* is another way of describing God's working through people. Spiritual healers claim to be channels of God's energy for the healing of the sick. They will take no credit for healings. As far as they are concerned, it is all God's power flowing through them.

Does being an instrument or channel for God have any significance today? I have no doubt about it! Daily, each one of us can transmit healing energy to another. We can do this by sending positive thoughts to one another or through the power of touch. To one degree or another each of us is an energy field. Research studies and Kirtulian photography has established that energy rings project out from each human being, the exception being a depressed person. As we share our energy or power with one another, we are being instruments of God. Pause and reflect a moment. What happens when you are in the presence of a positive and energetic person? Do you not feel lifted up and in some degree healed? A good way to begin giving your healing energy to another is to concentrate your full attention on that person.

A second aspect of Moses' intimate relationship with God is dialogue. What is a dialogue? A dialogue is a state of mutuality between two people fully participating in a flow of conversation. In this type of a conversation a range of feelings, such as anger, sadness, love, and joy, may be expressed. Before dialogue can take place, trust must be established. It is only with those whom we fully trust that the depths of the soul may be shared. Martin Buber calls authentic dialogue an I-Thou relationship, and it also includes one's encounter with the Divine Presence.[9]

There can be little question that Moses had an I-Thou relationship with God. Consider, for example, the following passage, "Thus the LORD used to speak to Moses face to face, as one speaks to a friend" (Ex. 33:11). Moses did not hesitate to share the depths of his soul with Yahweh (one of the Hebrew words for God). After the children of Israel had sinned by worshiping a golden calf, Moses came into the presence of God and cried out, "But now, if you will only forgive their sin—but if not, blot me out of the book that you have written" (Ex. 32:32).

In a healthy marriage, authentic dialogue is at the center. Partners respect the individuality of each other and call each other forth in terms of feelings, thoughts, dreams, visions, and creative ideas. Such a relationship becomes a rich spiritual experience because God is in it. Time and careful listening are essential. Dialogue with God is not different. It will call for an investment of time, solitude, and expectancy.

Will God respond to our questions? Will God speak in some way, shape, or form? God's part of the dialogue may be revealed in dreams, visions, scripture, intuitions, an inner voice, or through some mystical experience. The more we practice dialogue with God, the more intimate will be our relationship.

A final aspect of Moses' intimacy with God is luminosity. Luminosity is the radiance or glow that comes from being in the presence of God. The following passage is representative of Moses' luminosity. "The Israelites would see the face of Moses, that the skin of his face was shining; and Moses would put the veil on his face again, until he went in to speak with [the LORD]" (Ex. 34:35). Moses' face shone to the extent that the Israelites, probably because of fear, could not bear to look at his face. Whenever the radiant presence of God is encountered, directly or through angels, the initial response of humankind is usually fear. It is indeed awesome to encounter the brilliant light of God's presence, but when we come to experience that this light is love, we will inexorably be drawn toward it. Those who have had near-death experiences testify that the light they meet on the other side is such pure love that they feel completely accepted and at peace.

Being in God's luminous presence for even a few seconds is a life-changing experience. Though we may not have had the dramatic experience of Moses on Mount Horeb or Jesus at the transfiguration, we can nevertheless reflect God's radiance in one degree or another. The degree to which we reflect the glory of God will depend on how much time we spend in God's presence. Moses spent years in God's presence, and that is why his countenance glowed. How can each of us be a reflector of God's radiance? Simply by being aware of God's presence in all our activities and in the world about us. At the moment, my activity is writing. I feel the presence of God in my thoughts and in the words I form with my pen. The more I am aware of God's presence, the more I will reflect God's radiance. I am unable to say how much I reflect God's presence, but I am on the way.

Grandma Moses

The fourth spirituality model I have chosen is Grandma Moses, the folk artist. She is a striking example of one whose creativity blossomed in the ninth and tenth decades of life. She is a reminder to all seniors that creativity may be discovered and developed in the later years of life.

Anna Mary Robertson Moses was born in Greenwich, Washington County, New York, September 7, 1860. She grew up on a farm, one of ten children. At the age of twelve, Grandma Moses became a hired hand, tending children and doing household chores. This arrangement was not uncommon at that time, and it eased the situation her parents faced in providing for a large family.

Whatever schooling Grandma Moses received was in a one-room country school. On November 9, 1887, she married Salmon Moses, and they became tenant farmers in Shenandoah Valley, Virginia. Between 1887 and 1905 Grandma Moses bore ten children, half of which died in infancy. Hard times and hard work were borne patiently. We do not know how she responded to the loss of five infant children, but loss, grief, and tragedy did not appear in her artwork.

In 1905, the Moses family bought a farm at Eagle Bridge, New York. In this picturesque farm setting, after raising her children, Grandma Moses began her career as a folk artist. She painted to supplement her farm income and found it to be an enjoyable pastime. At first she did needlework pictures, distributing these at county fairs, rummage sales, and at the Thomas Rug Store in Hoosick Falls, New York. It was here, in 1934, that Louis Caldor, a civil engineer, took considerable interest in her work and arranged a display of her paintings at a New York Museum.

After a personal appearance in New York, under the caption of "what a farm wife has painted," and a tour of the U.S.A., Grandma Moses' career as a folk artist was established. She painted scenes of small towns, farms, changing seasons, rustic covered bridges, families enjoying Christmas, and rural churches. She proclaimed the values of church, family, nation, and community. Her basic honesty, good-heartedness, and generosity showed forth in her life and art.[10]

What accounted for the success and popularity of Moses' art? It was a combination of the artist, her work, and the times. In 1940 the values of the nation were under attack from both within and without. The paintings of Grandma Moses proclaimed the simple unchanged values that many American people desired and needed. Therefore, her paintings were much in demand.

Presidents Truman and Kennedy honored Grandma Moses, and Governor Rockefeller of New York proclaimed her birthday as Grandma Moses Day. Her artwork has been displayed in both Europe and Asia.

Grandma Moses was immune to the fame and self-importance. On one occasion she said, "If people want to make a fuss over me, I just let 'em. I am the same person now as I was before."[11] She was absolutely who she was, a simple country housewife. I have always believed that humility is one of the distinguishing virtues of a great person. Certainly Grandma Moses was such a person.

Grandma Moses continued to paint up to the end of her long life. *The Rainbow,* painted in 1961, was her last finished work. At this time she was more than one hundred years old! Grandma Moses' long life came to a close on December 13, 1961, at the age of 101. Her most creative artwork took place in the ninth, tenth, and eleventh decades of of her life–amazing!

What was the secret of Grandma Moses' creativity? Although I do not know the answer, I would like to set forth a possibility: Could it be that her artwork sprang from the creative spirit dwelling in the depths of her soul? Grandma Moses became the simple, honest, and unpretentious channel through which the inner creative spirit could work. Each one of us is endowed with a creative spirit, an inner spirit that seeks to express itself in a variety of ways. The purpose of the inner spirit is always to serve in one way or another. This inner spirit may lie dormant unless we are open and willing to test out whatever creative talent is buried within.

I have been pondering my response to Grandma Moses' paintings. Her paintings awaken my imagination and transport me back to pleasant images and fond memories. When I gaze at one of her farm scenes of gathering and staking hay, I am there. I am the farmer. I smell the freshly cut hay. What happens to me at such times is a pleasant retreat from the stress and strain of daily life. I feel relaxed and renewed.

If Grandma Moses' artwork produces such benefits for me, I have a hunch that it does this for many others. Grandma Moses' artwork will continue to endure because it touches on the permanent values of truth, honesty, and simplicity.

Morrie Schwartz

Morris Schwartz, the next spiritual model I have chosen, provides an opportunity to look at spirituality in the face of extreme disability, dying, and death. What does spirituality look like when dealing with a devastating terminal illness such as Amytrophic Lateral Sclerosis (ALS)? In a remarkable and touching book called *Tuesdays with Morrie,* Mitch Albom, author and a former student and close friend of Morrie, shares Morrie's insightful, courageous, and positive responses to a dreaded disease.[12]

Morrie was born of poor Russian immigrants in Manhattan's lower east side, in 1916. Morrie, his parents, and his brother David lived in a small, drab apartment in the back of a candy shop tended by his mother. Morrie's mother was frail and sick. After entering the hospital, a telegram was soon sent home informing the family that she had died. At this time Morrie was eight years old. He had to read the telegram to his father, who did not understand English. Morrie wept for his mother, but even more he longed for affection. His father was distant and silent and had no tenderness or affection to offer Morrie.

Times were hard. Morrie's father was out of a job most of the time. Morrie and his brother washed porch steps for a nickel. A bright spot came into Morrie's life in the person of Eva, his stepmother. She gave the hugs, kisses, and affection he desired. In addition, she stressed the importance of education.

When Morrie was a teenager, tragedy struck again when his father was accosted by two young men who demanded his money. Morrie's father ran from them, only to collapse and die of a heart attack several blocks down the street. Morrie last saw his father when he was called to the city morgue to identify his father's body.

Morrie now began the process of deciding what to do with his life. He did not want to go into law, because he disliked lawyers. Nor did he want to be a doctor, because he couldn't stand the sight of blood. Gradually he was drawn into teaching. He earned master's and doctoral degrees from the University of Chicago. In the early 1950s, he received a five-year grant to study mental illness at Chestnut Lodge in the Washington, D.C., area. This turned out to be a great learning laboratory in the dynamics of human behavior. In the late 1950s, Morrie became a professor of sociology at Brandeis University in Waltham, Massachusetts. Here, he taught courses in social psychology, group process, and mental illness. He became a favorite professor of students because he took a personal interest in each one. Grades were not important. It was helping the student learn and grow that mattered.

Morrie enjoyed family life. He and his wife, Charlotte, had two sons, Rob and Jon. Morrie made sure that much of the tenderness he had missed while growing up was openly shared in his family. Morrie's idea of a good time was dancing, going to a favorite restaurant, visiting, and exchanging ideas with friends. He was a full human being who could laugh and cry at a given moment.

In August 1994, after having symptoms of weakness in his legs, Morrie was diagnosed with ALS. He learned that his illness was terminal and that he might have only two years to live. Here, Morrie asked himself a crucial question: Do I wither and die, or do I make the best of my time left? He would not wither up nor be ashamed of dying. He would research his own dying and make it a final project.

During the months before his death at the end of 1995, Morrie lived out an in-depth spirituality. His courage and honesty were an inspiration to all, including those who saw him on Ted Koppel's *Nightline* television show. What was the content of Morrie's spirituality? From what I have been able to gather, it was based on the great commandment, which is to love God and to love one's neighbor as oneself (Lk. 10:27). Morrie was a spiritual eclectic and borrowed freely from Judaism, Christianity, Buddhism, and other sources.

I have compiled a list of Morrie's responses as he faced ALS, one of the most dreadful of all terminal diseases. There is much we can all learn as we thoughtfully and maybe painfully consider his responses.

First, Morrie responded with acceptance. The beginning point of dealing positively with any crisis is acceptance. But acceptance may not come quickly for all. There may be periods of denial, anger, and sadness. Acceptance may need to be renewed from time to time, and this is especially true as complications of a disease progress.

Acceptance is the only way I know to live with a disease.[13] Acceptance does not mean we like what is happening to us. It means we have come to a place of surrender. No longer do we have to spend energy in denial, anger, or sadness; rather, we can do as Morrie did and concentrate on loving relationships. It is doubtful that Morrie—or any of us—could maintain a state of acceptance without the support of family and friends.

One of the most prominent aspects of Morrie's acceptance was his early acceptance of dying and death. Morrie arranged for a living funeral with family, friends, and colleagues before his actual death. He spoke comfortably about his own dying, never forgetting that for him the experience of death was just around the corner.

Will I be able to be so frank and open about my own dying and death? I hope so. I am planning to face my own death openly and fully share what that experience is like to family and friends. Of course, this is presuming I have the time to do so.

Currently, I have a balance dysfunction, making it necessary for me to use canes for safe ambulation. As long as I accept my canes as essential to safe walking, I scarcely notice using them. However, when I see others walking around normally and I focus on what they can do that I can't do, I end up in a state of despair. Simple acceptance of the use of canes keeps me feeling good about myself with no need to envy others.

Mourning was another response of Morrie's. He allowed brief periods of mourning. He knew that too much mourning could turn into self-pity. I appreciate the delicate balance between too much mourning and too little. Too little mourning may keep sadness and tears suppressed, and too much may endanger emotional well-being. A good rule of thumb to follow is that when waves of loss and grief come, don't hold back. Let the tears come. I mourn over losses that have occurred in my body. I have lost eyesight to the point that I am classified as legally blind. For nine years I have not known the simple pleasures of driving a car. I mourn, but like Morrie, I keep it in the background. It is the foreground, and what is going on now, that gets my attention.

The more chronic the disease, the more there is to mourn about. When I learned I had diabetes, a disease that will not go away, my mourning was intense and full. But diabetes is usually not terminal if you take care of it. If one has a terminal disease such as Morrie had, it is that much harder to keep mourning properly balanced.

Detachment was Morrie's most useful response toward his death. As Morrie's ALS progressed to a point where breathing became difficult, fear would surge over him. It was then that he practiced detachment. Remarkably, he would simply step away and not let fear take over. He was able to disengage from harmful emotions. Attachment is the opposite of detachment. Can you imagine the consequences of attaching to a destructive emotion such as fear? Fear can lead to panic and in a few cases might even be fatal.

All of us can practice some form of detachment. I have found detachment in the midst of neuropathic pain by meditating on the Twenty-third Psalm. I visualize myself walking in green pastures and sitting by still waters. This helps me to take a break from my pain. All of us can benefit from learning how to detach. It can be therapeutic for the health of body, mind, and spirit to detach from pain, from a conflictual relationship, and from destructive emotions, stress, and strain.

Is dependency an acceptable response to illness, dying, and death? To Morrie, it not only became acceptable, but necessary. As his ALS progressed, there came a day when Morrie could not move his hands to feed himself or do bathroom chores. At these times, he saw himself as a helpless baby, completely dependent on others to meet basic needs. Instead of being ashamed, Morrie let himself be a baby once again.

Some people are very uncomfortable with being dependent on others. They want to continue being self-sufficient and in control. Perhaps they have been on the giving end, and now, through illness or disability, they find the receiving end more difficult to accept.

I have now come to accept dependency as a part of my lifestyle. I gladly accept rides and an arm to stabilize my walking. It was not always so. Initially, I was hesitant. I had to let go of pride and the feeling of not wanting to burden others. When I became open and straightforward about my dependency, I found that others were more than willing to help. However, I do not want others to do for me what I can do for myself, so I draw the line on becoming overly dependent. There are always a few dear souls who want to do more for me than is necessary. There may come a day when I am totally dependent, but that is a bridge I need not cross now.

Another way that Morrie responded to his crisis was to find meaning in his life. He found meaning in his family, friends, students, teaching, discussions, and in a hibiscus plant on his study window. Loving relationships with people and involvement in activities such as teaching kept Morrie going. Without such meaning, he could have given up and withered away. Mitch, a former student who visited Morrie on Tuesdays, is an example of one who provided meaning for Morrie's life. Morrie brightened each time Mitch visited. Morrie regarded these visits of such importance that he kept them up even when he could only manage a small whisper.

Meaning is the fuel that keeps life going. Without meaning, people give up and die. With meaning, people can live through the most difficult circumstances. Meaning stimulates the immune system and keeps host resistance strong.

In my case, I have found meaning to be a powerful antidote to depression. When I get downcast, I pause and reflect that my life has meaning and purpose. The spiritual dimension of this for me is that God has a meaning and purpose for my life. To keep going in spite of my physical limitations is to fulfill God's plan for my life.

Meanings need to be specific. Meanings need not be profound or earth shattering. Rather, they arise out of the simple things of life, such as taking a morning walk, taking care of a pet, visiting family and friends, or calling on someone immobile or shut-in. Avocations such as woodcarving, knitting, painting, and making pottery are also sources of meaning. Keep meaning going, and you stay alive. Let meaning go, and you wither up and die.

Morrie responded to his terminal illness with forgiveness. Forgiveness was critically important to Morrie. He did not want to die with any unfinished business, but as he was dying, he shed tears over a friend whom he had not forgiven even though he had had a couple of opportunities years earlier to do so. It was too late, as his friend had died. But it wasn't too late for Morrie to forgive himself and come to a state of inner harmony and peace. Here is Morrie's simple formula: "Forgive yourself before you die. Then forgive others."[14] As he reviewed his life, Morrie went on to say, "Forgive yourself for all the things you didn't do and all the things you should have done."[15] Forgiveness is not only important in the face of impending death, it needs to become a daily attitude.

Why is forgiveness so important? It provides a release from guilt. One of the sources of guilt is "if only." *If only I had done this or that while he was alive. If only I had been there when he died.* And the list goes on, and the burden of guilt becomes heavier and heavier.

Self-forgiveness is the process of letting go of the burden of over-responsibility. It is the realization and acceptance of being an imperfect and limited human being. When one no longer has to live up to self-imposed expectations, guilt fades away.

From a spiritual standpoint, forgiveness is the gift of a loving God. If God loves me so much that he has already pardoned my guilt, is there any reason that I should not pardon (forgive) myself?

Forgiveness puts the past in the past. It helps us to live in the present moment. Why does the past keep popping up, especially in unguarded moments when we are disengaged from daily tasks? Why is the life review phenomenon a common theme in seniors? The answer may well be that we are trying to come to terms with the past. There is a drive, perhaps unconscious, to make peace with the life we have lived.

In the early years of my ministry as a hospital chaplain, I was asked by a nurse to make a presurgical call on an eighty-year-old single lady. The threat and risk of major surgery had brought to the foreground a long-buried incident. The lady, whom I shall call Zelda, told me that at age twenty she had given birth to a child out of wedlock. This was a piece of her past for which she felt a deep sense of shame. In fact, she had kept it hidden for sixty years, never daring to share it with anyone. It was a relief for Zelda to make a confession, and through forgiveness of self, a piece of past history was resolved. I was happy to assist her in this process. Although she didn't look forward to her surgery, she was at peace with God.

It is hard, if not impossible, to live in the present moment if the past has not been settled. There are a myriad of ways to avoid dealing with the past. Need to keep busy, watching too much TV, and taking no time for silent reflection may be ways to avoid painful recollection of the past. But there usually comes a day, as it did for Zelda, when the past cannot be kept down. In one way or another, it will catch up. Forgiveness is the key to resolving the past and living in the present moment.

Another aspect of the power of forgiveness is the restoration of relationships. There is a classic story in the New Testament that Jesus tells about a young man who left home and squandered his inheritance in loose and careless living.[16] After having spent all of his money, he became desperate. He had no work, the land was in the grip of a famine, and he was very hungry. He went to work in the fields of a hog farmer, but he wasn't given anything to eat. As he was preparing to eat the pods given to the hogs, he thought of how lonely he had become and of how much better off he would be back at his father's home. Yes, he would take his chances. He would go back home, confess his sin, and hope to be restored to his father's household, even in the capacity of a hired servant. The young man greatly underestimated his father's capacity to forgive and restore. So happy was his father to have his lost son back home that he clothed him in royal garments, prepared a great feast, and invited all to join in a time of merrymaking. Thus did forgiveness end a long famine of alienation as the young man was restored to a loving relationship with his father.

Although this is an ancient story, it has a familiar ring to it. Which one of us, in one way or another, has not been alienated from family or friends? The way back is not always easy, as it may involve painful confession and swallowing one's pride. How easy is it to say "Forgive me" to a loved one we have hurt? It takes courage to admit our faults, but once this first step home is taken, the power of forgiveness will restore us to a full and joyful relationship. It is rare, indeed, that a loved one will not eventually grant forgiveness to the one who asks for it.

The point of Jesus' classic prodigal story is that our Heavenly Father is eager to embrace us and restore us to the home where once again we shall delight in his presence.

The spirituality models I have presented in this chapter have much to teach us about living a life of fullness. Consciously or unconsciously, each one of us is a spirituality model. In one way or another the spirituality model that we are will influence family, friends, and the community in which we live. The important thing is for each of us to be a unique and authentic model.

CHAPTER 3

Spirituality and Adversity

Ever since I was a boy going to grade school in a small town in central Kansas, I have been inspired and challenged by that state's motto, "Ad Astera Per Aspera." It means "to the stars, through difficulty." It is a fitting motto for this chapter, in the sense that adversities encountered in this life may become opportunities for learning, growth, and a life of fullness.

What does it mean to go through adversity? I see it as the facing and experiencing of a range of difficult and sometimes life-threatening events, of which the outcome is unpredictable.

Rites of Passage

A model to help us better understand the nature of adversity may be found in an ancient practice called Rites of Passage.[1] Cultural anthropologists have brought this concept to our attention in modern times. The first stage in rites of passage is separation. It involves movement from the familiar to the unfamiliar. It is a leaving of what has been dependable to facing a world of uncertainty. One is separated from daily rituals that have brought order and meaning to life. Loneliness, anxiety, and fear may be a part of this phase.

For the tribesman of old it meant separation from his village, parents, friends, and familiar rituals, and to be alone in the surrounding jungle or forest. It was all part of an initiation ceremony and a passage into adulthood.

Adversity, in one degree or another, thrusts one into a time of separation. When diagnosed with diabetes, I was quickly propelled into a frightening world of insulin shots, sugar testing, and a diabetic meal plan. Gone were my days of eating what I wanted and when I wanted it. Familiar ways were gone, and all was new, different, and confusing.

The second stage is no-man's-land, or being betwixt and between. This stage is a wilderness experience accompanied by confusion, bewilderment, and despair. Identity is lost. One may ask, What will become of me? Will I be crushed by this adversity? Will it be the death of me, or will I recover? Trials and turmoil may come. One senses he or she, like Job, is being put through a severe test. The outcome is by no means certain.

In the midst of struggle there comes an encounter with the Holy. In Native American tradition the Holy may be encountered as an eagle. The Holy may also be identified as God or Christ. The Holy One is recognized as all-powerful, not bound by time or space, and as one who may guide us to solid ground. At this point, a time of life review and reflection may occur. What mistakes have I made? How can I live a more giving and loving life? In Native American tradition a mythic story that is widely known can give strength and courage to the individual. Now there is hope of making it out of the wilderness.

In my struggle to face and accept diabetes, I can relate to all aspects of the traveler in no-man's-land. I was in no-man's-land for a considerable period of time, struggling with identity and being caught up in despair. This journey taught me valuable lessons about the meaning and purpose of my life.

The last stage in rites of passage is transformation. The reflections that began in no-man's-land have now taken shape as valuable lessons. Maintenance of a vital relationship with the Holy Being, with community, and with oneself are among the most important lessons. A new identity and name are often bestowed. For example, Jacob, after wrestling all night long with a holy being, was given the name Israel. His life was forever changed by the powerful encounter with an emissary of God (Gen. 32:24–32).

In the case of the tribesman, all lessons learned in the wilderness are discussed and affirmed by the elders of the tribe. A new name and new clothes are given as signs of passage into adulthood. The young man is accepted as a warrior who can join in hunting and battles and can take on adult responsibilities.

When I emerged from the no-man's-land of denying and struggling with diabetes, I took on a new name and new responsibilities. I now called myself a wounded healer. I could now shape my experience for the benefit and healing of others as well as myself. I endured the gloomy predictions of some medical personnel, had a few close encounters with death, and faced some difficult diabetic complications. These adversities have brought about a transformation in me. My life has a deeper meaning and purpose as a result of going through the rites of passage. It is not a once-for-all-time event. With the advent of a new adversity, I expect once again to tread the passageways, though the guideposts will be more familiar.

One may look at the campus of a retirement community and observe seniors engaged in various activities and conclude that there is no adversity there; but such an observation may be superficial, for adversity has many faces and forms. Adversity has both an inward and an outward face. The outward face can be seen in various forms of illness and disability. Such limitations are easy to see, but who can clearly behold the inward face of stress, loss and grief, and emotional and mental troubles? In one degree or another the inward face of adversity may remain hidden and suppressed. The polite and ritualistic "How are you?" that most of us use nearly everyday seldom touches the hurt and pain that may be concealed within. Only trustful dialogue with a friend or counselor will call forth inward pain and hurt.

All outward forms of illness have inward components of hurt, emotional pain, and sometimes depression and despair. While medicine addresses the outward dimension, it is equally important that the inward dimension be addressed.

Caring for and Feeling with the Dying

I remember a Native American woman in her late sixties whom I visited at a convalescent center while doing volunteer pastoral care ministry as a retiree. She was a double amputee, both legs having been removed above the knees. In addition, she had to go for renal dialysis three times a week. Often, when walking into her room, I was greeted by a blank stare, as though her thoughts had carried her away into another time and place. She didn't complain, nor did she have much to say, but it was clear that the spiritual ministry I brought her touched a deep chord of inner faith. She would give me a faint smile and shake my hand before I left her room. She had few visitors. Occasionally, a grandson would visit from the reservation. I think my visits took away some of her loneliness.

One day I stepped into an empty room, wondering what had become of her. A pang of grief struck me when I learned that she had died during the night. Diabetes and its complications had run its full course with this dear little Native American lady. Her death was a healing and a graduation to better things. I paused and reflected. Somewhere I heard a bell tolling for me. Would diabetes do this to me? I hoped not, but I had no guarantees. It was no wonder I had a deep empathy for this lady.

I will discuss two more forms of adversarial illness, namely, multiple sclerosis and Alzheimer's disease.

My friend Alan has the slowly progressive type of multiple sclerosis.[2] Since being diagnosed seventeen years ago, he has gradually lost his muscular functioning to the point that he cannot feed or take care of himself at all. At first he was able to be at home and get around in a motorized chair, but now he lies helpless on a hospital bed in a nursing home. He took early retirement as a professor, mentor, and researcher in the field of chemical engineering. His specialty was doing research in crystallization. Many graduate students sought out his tutelage. Alan loved academic life and its intellectual challenges, but now it has all been lost and remains only as a memory. How does one deal with such incredible helplessness and loss?

Alan has at least three things that keep him going: the support and love of family and friends, spiritual therapy, and ice cream. His wife and three children keep in close contact, and every week a friend brings in a movie video to watch with him. Spiritual therapy is offered through friends who share scripture and prayer. This morning as I was writing these lines, I paused to make a phone call to Alan. (He has a special telephone hookup that does not require the use of his hands.) I shared two verses of scripture about how God's love, in Christ, remains with us regardless of the bitter circumstances that may engulf us. There was a silence on the other end of the line, followed by a deliberate, "Thank you." I know that Alan drinks deeply of the eternal water of life that comes his way. He knows that someday he will have a spiritual body beyond the reach of crippling disease.

One day when I asked Alan what he most enjoyed in his day, he said, "Ice cream." So every day my friend enjoys a dish of ice cream. If it makes his life just a little more complete, why not?

How does Alan's condition impact me? I wonder how I could deal with such utter helplessness. Would I be able to keep going?

I am also impacted by a profound sense of gratefulness. Although I have significant limitations, I can still read, write, and get around with the use of canes. I am also motivated to reach out to others before the time comes when I can no longer work.

A disease that is becoming increasingly common among older Americans is Alzheimer's. This disease has been increasingly diagnosed for about two decades, and four million Americans are afflicted with it.[3] It is a degenerative and progressive brain disorder that affects memory, thinking, personality, and behavior. At this time there is no cure or effective treatment.

What is it like to have a loved one suffer with Alzheimer's? To find out, I decided to interview Fred[4] and gain insights from his firsthand knowledge and experience. Fred's wife has been diagnosed with Alzheimer's for ten years and is now a patient in a skilled nursing care unit. He visits her on a daily basis, but feels he has gradually lost the wife he once knew. One of the hardest things for Fred to bear is the continual reminders of loss, such as his wife's not knowing who he is and her inability to communicate as she once did. One of the most difficult things for Fred is that there is no apparent resolution to his grief; it goes on and on. When someone dies, the grief may eventually be resolved, but with Alzheimer's, mourning goes on, for there are constant reminders each time you visit your loved one. I am not saying it is impossible to resolve grief with a loved one having Alzheimer's, but it is certainly more difficult.

Sometimes Fred's spouse is hostile toward him. Other times she thinks that it is Fred, and not she, who has a problem. Fred's wife is quite often trying to find her way back home again. She wants to go back to that which is familiar and secure. Sometimes she has scary nighttime hallucinations and paranoid delusions and can be easily frightened.

How does Fred respond to his wife and all the changes she has gone through? Sometimes he expresses his grief by having a good cry. In general, Fred is tolerant, understanding, caring, and loving. He desires to do what he can to brighten up his wife's life. He is thankful for rare moments of lucidity when she seems to recognize him.

As I was concluding my interview with Fred, I asked what kept him going. Without hesitation he replied, "I don't think I could make it without prayer." I have the feeling that Fred has developed an intimate and trusting relationship with God. Fred not only realizes support from a loving God, but he also feels the support of family, friends, and caregivers. Fred has not become bitter, resentful, or withdrawn as a result of adversities that have come his way. He is an open, caring, and kind man. In the more than one year I have known him, I have found that he lives life on a spiritual plane. Could this be one of his keys, if not the major one, of creatively coping with his wife's Alzheimer's disease?

Understanding Pain

I move next to a discussion of pain, for it is frequently a companion to illness and adversity. Undoubtedly, pain is one of the most difficult of all human experiences to face and go through. At one time or another, all of us will have to deal with some form of pain. Pain is a universal experience, and it has been so since the dawn of civilization.

In any discussion of pain, the first question that comes to mind is, What is the meaning of pain? Pain is an experience that affects the whole person—body, mind, and spirit. Throbbing, stabbing, and burning physical sensations that come from illness or accident may also register in the mind as fear, anxiety, or depression, and in the spirit as feeling forsaken by God. In the darkest hours of pain, while being crucified on a cross, even Jesus felt forsaken by God.[5]

Pain may be acute or chronic. Acute pain is usually of limited duration, and one knows that after a period of time it will go away. This is not so with chronic pain. It may persist for months and years. As I write these lines, I am recovering from hernia surgery. After the anesthetic wore off, I became aware of a sharp, disturbing pain. I was able to get some relief with pain medication, but any strain in the surgical area still felt very uncomfortable. Now that I am in my fifth post-operative day, the pain is considerably less. In acute pain there is usually hope and light at the end of the tunnel because one knows that the pain will go away. My mind and spirit were only slightly ruffled. Acute pain is tolerable because it will heal with or without medical treatment. Unfortunately, that is not the case with much chronic pain.

Chronic pain is any pain that lasts more than three months and is not helped by medical treatment. Diseases and conditions associated with chronic pain include arthritis, back pain, cancer, neck pain, diabetic neuropathy, migraine headaches, and neuralgias. These are only a few of a long list of diseases associated with chronic pain.[6]

What is it like to deal with chronic pain? Speaking from my own experience, as one who deals with diabetic neuropathy, it can be a frustrating and maddening ordeal. Pain that persists, hour after hour, and through the night, puts a severe test on emotional and spiritual sanity. There is no known remedy for diabetic neuropathy. I feel fortunate that the attacks of painful tingling in my lower legs and feet are only periodic.

According to a *Guideposts* article written in August 1999, there are fifty million chronic pain sufferers in the U.S. What do chronic pain sufferers go through? How are their lives affected? Following is a partial list of the side effects of chronic pain:

- Guilt
- Depression
- Isolation
- Anger
- Self-pity
- Feelings of punishment
- Why did it happen to me?
- Where is God?
- Fatigue
- Job change or job dysfunction
- Financial strains
- Thoughts about dying
- Suicide
- Family routine disrupted
- High divorce rate (70 percent to 80 percent)

Responding to Pain

Although there are many side effects to pain, they need not control our lives or turn us into victims. Because we are endowed with free will, we can choose a path that gives us power over pain. In Dr. Neal Olshan's useful book *Power Over Your Pain Without Drugs,* he presents a plan to modify and control pain. The most important elements are as follows:[7]

- Relaxation techniques
- Self-hypnosis
- Autogenics
- Pain control imagery
- Exercise

How do these methods control pain? They stimulate the release of endorphins, nature's built-in painkiller, to reduce and in some cases completely remove pain. How powerful are endorphins? The following story of a Vietnam helicopter pilot illustrates the point. Randy was flying into a clearing in the dense foliage of a Vietnam jungle when his helicopter was jolted by a blast of sniper fire. His co-pilot was instantly killed, and Randy felt the searing pain of bullet wounds in his left leg. Randy reasoned that if he did not pick up the wounded soldiers and take them to an aid station, no one else would. Once that decision was made, Randy's pain stopped. Ten minutes later, after landing at the aid station, the pain returned and Randy had to be carried off the helicopter.

What was it that caused Randy's pain to stop while he rescued the wounded soldiers? In this emergency, Randy's brain had released endorphins that set aside the pain long enough for Randy to safely fly back to the aid station.

For those who suffer from chronic pain, it is very good news that there are methods to release endorphins that will control pain. For those interested in detailed descriptions of the five methods of pain control mentioned by Dr. Olshan, please consult chapter sixteen of his book *Power Over Your Pain Without Drugs.*

A most remarkable account of how pain can be faced and controlled is found in Reynolds Price's book *A Whole New Life.*[8] At age fifty-one, Price was stricken with spinal cord cancer that created severe pain and left him a paraplegic. He went through twenty-five radiation treatments, which were more damaging than helpful, and three surgeries, which ultimately succeeded in removing the cancerous tissue. These procedures did nothing to alleviate the pain that continued unabated in his neck, shoulders, back, and legs. There were times when Price wondered if he was dying. The ordeal of relentless burning and scalding pain left him weary, exhausted, and sometimes despairing. Yet in the midst of it all he did not give up hope. The hope came through having steadfast supporting and loving friends; writing novels, poems, and plays; teaching; and engaging spirituality. Especially significant to Price was a vision of meeting with Jesus on the shore of the Sea of Galilee.

In this vision Jesus invited Price into waist-deep water and poured water over his head, saying, "Your sins are forgiven." Price followed Jesus and inquired if he would be cured. Jesus turned and said, "That too."[9]

This powerful meeting with Jesus was to sustain and inspire Price over many months of arduous medical treatments, high levels of pain, and dark, confused periods when healing seemed an unreachable goal. The vision also brought a feeling that God was near and had a special interest in his situation. In repeated hospitalizations and bouts with side effects of strong drugs, Price doubted his vision but never gave it up. What Price experienced in doubting the vision is a normal human response to adversity. What one of us has not had such a response?

What is important to emphasize here is that visitations of God or Jesus are not uncommon in times of trouble. The key is to be open and aware of such occurrences. In addition, directing heartfelt questions to the Divine Presence may one day (or night) bring forth an answer.

As another anchor in the time of storm, Price found himself returning to the faith of his parents and his early religious training. He found comfort in prayer, and often prayed, "Thy will be done." He had communion brought to his bedside and felt a sense of God's presence near him.

At this point a summary of the elements that brought healing to Price will serve to condense a long story:

Rehabilitation Training

In rehabilitation training Price learned skills to help him function more independently. In learning to do as much for himself as possible, he gained more control of life and bolstered self-esteem and self-confidence. From my own experience I know how important it is to be actively involved in a progressive rehab program. In my case I spent eighteen months learning balancing skills. After each outpatient session I came away feeling good about my accomplishments.

Most significantly, doing something for yourself keeps hope alive.

Support System

The support of family was a core element in Price's healing. His brother, Bill, and cousin, Marcia, provided encouragement and live-in support for weeks. Colleagues and students also provided vital companionship and live-in support. Price's praise for the loving care of family and friends occurs again and again throughout his book. They were all lifelines, providing transportation, preparing meals, and being present day and night to render assistance.

Medical Care

Although Price felt that some of the medical professionals attending him were aloof and distant, he came to feel close to Allen Friedman, his surgeon. The expert skills and compassionate care of Dr. Friedman became an essential factor in Price's healing. A key in the healing was the trustful relationship that developed. Who can be healed without trust? Full trust enables healing energy to flow, blessing both giver and receiver.

Work

It is impossible to overestimate the great healing effect of work to Price. "I will work as long as I have work to do, and work as long as I have life."[10] By concentrating on a piece of creative work, such as a sketch, novel, poem, or play, it became a vehicle in which pain was set aside. It took Price three long years to train his mind to set pain aside. Price learned to ignore pain so that he could say, "It is nothing."[11] A very amazing statement! Later, I will go into methods that made it possible for Price to make this claim. I have found that my work, which is now writing, demands such total concentration that I am unaware of pain sensations in my legs and feet. Focusing the mind away from pain, when involved in a compelling activity, is a major key to shutting down the pain.

Mind Control

Price found that biofeedback and hypnosis were effective therapies for mind control. At first he resisted both methods, but he soon found both to be of tremendous value in detaching from pain. In biofeedback he learned to raise the temperature of one hand while the other hand stayed cool. The whole idea that he could control areas of the body provided assurance that he could help himself.

Learning the art of hypnosis from a hypnotherapist required eight weeks, and it turned out to be an exciting and worthwhile venture. A month after the sessions, Price was able to set pain aside.

Although I am a beginner, I can vouch for the power of hypnosis to set pain aside. Why is this so? Hypnosis opens the door to the unconscious mind, which in turn acts on suggestions given during hypnotic trance. Even if you are not a pain sufferer, learning hypnosis can assist you in becoming healthier and more in control of your life.

Rebirth

What Price's concept of rebirth meant to him was letting go of the old life (the one lived before his illness) and embracing his new lifestyle. As far as he was concerned, the old life was dead, and he had been reborn into a whole new life. Several things were different about Price's new lifestyle—namely patience, listening, and creativity.

His patience came as a result of four long years of struggle to be healed. The ability to listen developed as he himself was listened to during the long ordeal of his illness.

Interestingly, Price's creativity increased during and after his illness. From 1984–1994 Price wrote thirteen books, an amazing feat.[12] Few authors can match this productivity.

I find Price's concept of rebirth applicable to my life. Dealing with several limitations myself, I find it tempting to go back and capture yesterday's unlimited lifestyle, but yesterday is gone and it will not come back. Would I want it to come back? By no means. Therefore, I am letting the old go and embracing my whole new life. I am being reborn to a new self, one with more acceptance, understanding, empathy, and peace. I believe all rebirth is a spiritual process. If we are willing, God is shaping us into more whole persons through our adversities.

Suffering and Adversity

The word *suffer* is a household word, often falling from the lips of many people. There are pain sufferers, grief sufferers, those who suffer physical and mental illnesses, and those who suffer from broken hearts or broken spirits.

What do people mean when they use the word *suffer*? What is suffering? In the discussion to follow, I hope to provide a perspective on suffering that will be both enlightening and useful.

I will begin with a biblical perspective. In Old Testament literature, the book of Job is an outstanding example of the problems, opportunities, and mysteries involved in suffering. One of the main problems for Job was that of justice and morality. How could God allow severe affliction and pain to come to his servant who shuns evil and is righteous and blameless? But Job's question apparently falls on deaf ears. Therefore, Job plunges deeper into fear, anxiety, dread, suicidal thoughts, and despair, cursing the day he was born. Job can find no solace in sleep, saying, "When I lie down I say, 'When shall I rise?' / But the night is long, / and I am full of tossing until dawn" (Job 7:4).

For Job (and for us), suffering has no easy answers. Job wants to make some sense out of the senselessness of his suffering. How will he find meaning in the calamity that has befallen him? Somehow, and in some way, he must meet with Yahweh (God), but this is no easy task. Who is he, a mere mortal, to meet with the omnipotent Creator of the universe?

Here, Job raises at least two valuable issues for our consideration. The first has to do with what we will do with our sufferings. To whom will we turn? Job chooses to turn toward God, and in this choice he ultimately comes to a place of peace and hope. But if we mortals do turn to God, will the mighty Creator pay any attention? The answer to this second issue is yes, but God may come in ways we do not understand. If we remember that God's ways are not our ways, then the mysterious way God meets us in our sufferings will not appear so strange. What is important to remember in the time of suffering is the knowledge that God will meet with those who turn to God. In the final chapter of the book of Job, Job describes his meeting with God: "I had heard of you by the hearing of the ear, / but now my eye sees you" (Job 42:5).

Can suffering provide opportunities for learning and growth? From a biblical perspective, it is safe to say that the core purpose of suffering is to move humankind toward a greater spiritual awareness and transformation. The opportunities for growth through suffering are not limited to the book of Job, but can be drawn from different Old and New Testament sources. Some opportunities suffering presents for learning are as follows.

Testing

Just as running a race provides an opportunity to test speed and endurance, suffering may be an opportunity to test such qualities as faith, obedience, and integrity. An example may be found in Abraham, who was called on to sacrifice his son Isaac on Mount Moriah (Gen. 22:1–13). Paul endured beatings, persecutions, shipwrecks, slander, trials, imprisonments (2 Cor. 11:23–28), and ultimately death. Jesus of Nazareth faced the ultimate test. He was betrayed by one of his own disciples, scourged, beaten, falsely accused, spat on, ridiculed, and finally put to death by crucifixion (Lk. 22:47–23:46)

What will be our response when tests come our way? If we can endure the tests and finish the race, we will gain courage, strength, patience, and joy.

Purification

Purification is being able to burn away and remove the clutter of things that block our hearts and minds from seeing God. If we center our lives on power, pleasure, fortune, and material possessions, suffering can soon teach us that these things have no lasting value. Purification is the process of burning away or cleansing the impurities that have crept into our lives. Thus, in the Old Testament, the prophet Malachi speaks of God as a "refiner's fire and...fullers' soap" (Mal. 3:2). In addition, God is pictured as "a refiner and purifier of silver"(3:3). As silver is purified, so will God purify God's people. Jesus conveys a similar idea in the beatitude that states, "Blessed are the pure in heart, for they will see God" (Mt. 5:8). Who are the pure in heart? They are those who give undivided attention to God, or as Søren Kierkegaard put it, they are those who will one thing. Purgatory, as presented in *Dante's Inferno,* is a redemptive process. It is a place to be purged and cleansed before entering Paradise.

Not everyone who suffers is purified. One must be willing to pass through "the refiner's fire" and be scrubbed with "fullers' soap."

Insight

Insight is an "aha" or "eureka" experience in which one sees a hitherto clouded aspect of life in full light. Job had this idea when he stated, "what is hidden, [God] brings forth to light" (Job 28:11b, NKJV). The psalmist speaks in a similar vein when he prays to be known and searched by God so that he might know his hidden faults (Ps. 139:23–24). Jesus wisely counsels that we take the log out of our own eye before we attempt to take the speck out of our brother's eye (Mt. 7:3–5). All of these passages have one theme in common—namely, that we come to see ourselves as we are. How does suffering bring us to a place of insight? In my experience it has helped me to review my life and ask questions such as, How have I participated in the suffering that has come upon me? To what extent have my attitudes and behavior been a precursor to suffering? What kind of person am I? What is my life all about? Through suffering I have come to see myself more clearly and to take responsibility for choices I have made. To see ourselves as we are, without projecting blame on others or on God, is the gift that insight brings to our lives.

Joy

How can suffering be an opportunity to experience joy? Most sufferers, and I include myself, would not say that suffering is joyful. On the contrary, most of us would say that it is painful. The psalmist, however, sees that joy may be born out of anguish; he declares, "Weeping may linger for the night, / but joy comes with the morning" (Ps. 30:5b). Paul speaks in a similar vein when he declares, "I consider that the sufferings of this present time are not worth comparing with the glory about to be revealed to us" (Rom. 8:18).

A word about the timing of joy: there is a joy that comes at the end of suffering, and there is certainly a day when our sufferings will cease. This may be at the end of a lifetime or at the end of a particular period of suffering. The joy will come as a sense of relief and from the triumph of endurance through a period of suffering. However, all joy is not to be postponed to the end. There is a here-and-now joy that transcends suffering. James picks up this theme in the following verse: "My brothers and sisters, whenever you face trials of any kind, consider it nothing but joy" (Jas. 1:2).

I can identify with both types of joy—the joy that comes in the here and now and the joy that comes at the end.

Character Building

Did you ever stop to think that suffering is a character builder? This is how Paul says character is built: "We also boast in our sufferings, knowing that suffering produces endurance, and endurance produces character, and character produces hope" (Rom. 5:3-4).

What is character? It is the quality of a person who has endured the tests of time, is trustworthy, is dependable, and will not hide when the day of battle comes. Those with character are the veterans who have fought the battles of life and have prevailed. One whose character has been built through suffering no longer asks why he or she is going through suffering. Now he or she knows that the suffering has purpose. The suffering is not a waste of time, nor is it futile, but rather it builds patience, endurance, perseverance, character, and hope. Moreover, it may serve as an encouragement and model to those who walk the path of suffering or who will one day walk that path.

Perhaps the brightest gem that character produces is hope. As long as hope is present, an individual keeps going. If hope is lost, in any given ordeal or trial, the individual will soon decline and eventually die. In whatever trials I have gone through, hope is that bright star that keeps me going. Hope has become so fundamental to me that I cannot live a day or pass through a night without it.

Suffering, from a biblical perspective, teaches us that it is purposeful, and it provides opportunities for learning and growth. In particular, it is an opportunity for testing, purification, insight, joy, and character building. Suffering may raise issues of justice and morality, and there is also an element in suffering that is mysterious. Suffering is more than a response to physical pain. It is also a response to emotional, mental, spiritual, and interpersonal pain.

Dread is the feeling that one may not be able to make it through a long night of suffering. Dread is not an uncommon experience. From time to time, most human beings face and go through some form of dread. My greatest dread would be the loss of my wife. Besides the pain of loss and separation, I would have a most difficult time surviving without her enabling presence. I would hope to pass through my dread and not get stuck in it. Faith is my strong ally and antidote to dread.

Perhaps the most severe form of suffering is despair. Why is this so? Because despair is an experience in which all hope is lost. In the concentration camps of World War II, prisoners could withstand torture, but not the loss of hope. The torment of despair is to not be able to die.[13] In this sense, suicide is an attempt to terminate despair. Despair may be the embodiment of the dark night of the soul, for in this situation one has lost the light of God.

Can any good come out of despair? If the utter helplessness, emptiness, and meaninglessness of despair can drive us to find a faith foundation, then it will have served us well. To take it one more step, our hope may lie in embracing despair. In embracing despair, we are embracing the unacceptable within ourselves. In this transaction we claim a lost part of ourselves. Could this be the internal process by which hope may come out of despair? Is this the way that God works to transform despair into hope?

Interpersonal suffering occurs when one feels cut off from family, friends, and caregivers. I have seen this happen with hospitalized terminal cancer patients. The cutoff happens when authentic dialogue ceases. Dialogue is the fundamental process of sharing in-depth thoughts and feelings. It is a two-way process that results in feeling understood, accepted, and loved. Loss of body image and loss of self-esteem are major factors in a terminal cancer patient's withdrawal and isolation. These feelings may be accelerated when a physician seldom visits as death approaches.

What can be done to unblock emotional cutoff and interpersonal suffering? Henry was a man in his mid-sixties who had just retired. He and his wife were looking forward to an enjoyable retirement. During a series of medical tests, Henry was found to have inoperable cancer. When I stepped into his hospital room one afternoon, Henry told me the bad news, and that he did not want his wife to know about his inoperable cancer. If Henry had followed this course of secrecy, he would have suffered emotional cutoff from his most primary and important relationship. As he was helped to see the consequences of such concealment, he elected to come out into the open. Henry took on the pain and tears of open sharing, and in so doing avoided the greater pain of isolation. Of course, there would have come a day when Henry's wife would have found out, but in the meantime they would have missed the intimacy, support, and closeness that resulted from their sharing.

Some individuals choose to suffer alone. They prefer to keep their feelings and thoughts to themselves. Although I feel that this is a path of loneliness, I respect the right of each person to choose his or her own path. I have seen families at a time of crisis with so much division, brokenness, and resentment that each family member is an island of isolation.

Suffering resulting from broken relationships, withdrawal, and self-concealment is perhaps the hardest of all sufferings to bear because it denies our need for human relatedness.

In the midst of suffering, there are three gems of wisdom that help provide perspective, strength, and comfort. They are as follows:

- This, too, will pass.
- Many others have lived through these sufferings before me.
- There is someone who knows and cares about my sufferings.[14]

The common thread is faith—a faith that sees an end to suffering; a faith that believes if others have made it through a time of suffering, "I also can get through it"; and a faith that sees a loving God who knows and cares.

In our discussion of suffering we have talked mostly about involuntary suffering–suffering we did not choose, at least not on a conscious level. There is, however, a type of suffering in which one deliberately chooses to be involved in a work or mission that will bring about suffering or perhaps death. This is voluntary suffering, and there are many outstanding examples recorded in history. Jesus took upon himself the role of a suffering servant and gave his life as a ransom for many. His apostles, Peter, James, and John, followed the model of Jesus, suffering many persecutions in order that others be liberated from sin and bondage. Joan of Arc defied the religious authorities of her day, giving up her life so that the common person might know the simple path to salvation. In modern times, Martin Luther King, Jr., suffered ridicule, beatings, harassment, and finally death, that black people would gain their civil rights and become free people.

Voluntary suffering is suffering of the highest order. In one degree or another, all may participate by being willing to suffer something for the benefit of others. It is for those who are not satisfied to stand on the sidelines, but are willing to invest time, energy, blood, sweat, and tears for the benefit of a person or a society.

Stress and Adversity

If stress wears one down and results in physical or emotional illness, it can be looked at as an adversary or a foe. However, if one can keep stress within normal limits, manage it, and use it well, it can be a friend.

To begin, let us look at a rationale for stress. Why do we have it? It is not possible to live in today's world without experiencing stress. Noise pollution, air pollution, waiting in traffic lines, robberies, violence, murders, mass media, and calamities of nature are just a few of the stressors that bombard us. No matter how much we may try to ignore or avoid stress, it is part of our world. While we cannot change the fact of stress, we can choose how we will respond to it. If we choose a positive response to stress, it will in the long run build us into stronger persons, ever more capable of handling it well.

Stress and Seniors

Are seniors immune from stress? Whether living independently or with family or in a retirement community, seniors continue to face stress in one form or another. In some instances stress may even increase, especially as health issues become more prominent.

For some seniors retirement is a stressor. The loss of income, social relationships, prestige, status, purpose, and a place to go become difficult adjustments. The inability to let go of the workplace and adopt a new lifestyle is where the stress enters in. Hanging on to what has been, but will be no more, can create a great deal of stress. For some seniors retirement may be an immediate welcome change, but for others it may be a process of gradually letting go. Some say that they have flunked retirement, usually meaning they have gone back to work again. Perhaps this is a way of easing the change from work to a retired lifestyle. Some may enjoy working on a part-time basis more than being retired. For me, retirement has presented an opportunity for reading, study, writing, and volunteer pastoral care ministry. Retirement has set me free from time deadlines, a former stressor. Initially, retirement did create stress for me as it brought about a profound change in my lifestyle. No longer would I be actively engaged with patients, families, students, and hospital staff in the stimulating milieu of a university medical center.

The one constant in the life of a senior is change. Much of our stress takes place around life-changing events.

It is time now to inquire into the nature of stress. What is stress? In order to answer this question, it is necessary to go back to the ground-breaking research of Dr. Hans Selye. Dr. Selye coined the word *stress* as a way of identifying the physical changes that take place in the body due to external and internal stimulation. He clearly demonstrated that stress has its effects on body systems, such as the cardiovascular, respiratory, and musculoskeletal systems and the endocrine glands. He showed that stress, over a period of time, can wear down these systems so that the weakest link in the system may break down. The result is lowered resistance and immunity, culminating in some form of illness. Selye identified three stages in how stress works on the body: alarm, resistance, and exhaustion.[15]

I will briefly discuss each stage. Alarm is the body's initial reaction to a crisis situation such as serious illness, death of a spouse, divorce, or a calamity of nature. The body systems all mobilize to meet the emergency. The sympathetic nervous system reacts with fear, anxiety, or even panic. If the stress lasts too long or is repeated, the resistance stage may be reached. In this stage the body mobilizes to resist. Prolonged resistance places the body under severe strain, which is analogous to keeping a brake pedal on a car continuously depressed, eventually wearing out the brake pad. If the stress continues for months or years without abatement, a point of exhaustion may be reached. In this third stage body reserves are used up, and it may herald the onset of a physical or mental illness.

Dr. Selye's research into the physiology of stress can serve us very well by making us aware of what our bodies go through during times of stress. Increased awareness can help us see the need for finding ways to reduce and minimize stress.

Another way of seeing how stress affects us is through the concept of life-changing events. In order to see how life changes affect people, psychiatrists Thomas H. Holmes and Richard Rahe developed a social readjustment scale. They ranked the events according to the time it takes to adjust to them. They found that the death of a spouse was the most difficult adjustment, so it was rated at 100 life changing units (LCUs). Near the bottom of the list of forty-three items was Christmas, which received 12 LCUs. The total LCUs accumulated in a year determines your risk of experiencing a health change. A score of 150–199 may be considered a mild life crisis, with a 37 percent chance of worsening health in the coming year; 200–299 is moderate, with a 50 percent chance of worsening health; and 300 or higher is considered a major life crisis, with an 80 percent chance of illness. There are vast differences in how individuals bear up or break down under stress. Not all who score over 300 will develop an illness, while some who score in a range of 150–199 may become ill. For those who are not familiar with the social readjustment rating scale, and who may want to check their personal scores, I will include a copy of the scale. Circle each LCU you have experienced in the last twelve months and total your score.[16]

Social Readjustment Rating Scale

Rank	Life event	LCU value
1.	Death of spouse	100
2.	Divorce	73
3.	Marital separation	65
4.	Jail term	63
5.	Death of close family member	63
6.	Personal injury or illness	53
7.	Marriage	50
8.	Fired from job	47
9.	Marital reconciliation	45
10.	Retirement	45
11.	Change in health of family member	44
12.	Pregnancy	40
13.	Sex difficulties	39
14.	Gain of new family member	39
15.	Business readjustment	39
16.	Change in financial state	38
17.	Death of close friend	37
18.	Change to different line of work	36
19.	Change in number of arguments with spouse	35
20.	Mortgage over $10,000	31

21.	Foreclosure of mortgage or loan	30
22.	Change in responsibilities at work	29
23.	Son or daughter leaving home	29
24.	Trouble with in-laws	29
25.	Outstanding personal achievement	28
26.	Wife begins or stops work	26
27.	Begin or end school	26
28.	Change in living conditions	25
29.	Revision of personal habits	24
30.	Trouble with boss	23
31.	Change in work hours or conditions	20
32.	Change in residence	20
33.	Change in schools	20
34.	Change in recreation	19
35.	Change in church activities	19
36.	Change in social activities	18
37.	Mortgage or loan less than $10,000	17
38.	Change in sleeping habits	16
39.	Change in number of family get-togethers	15
40.	Change in eating habits	15
41.	Vacation	13
42.	Christmas	12
43.	Minor violations of the law	11

In telephone interviews, twenty-four seniors living in a retirement community identified twenty-nine different stressors. They are as follows:

- Health changes and concerns
- Loss and grief
- Caregiver stress
- Financial concerns
- Family crises
- Survival after death of spouse
- Overactivity
- Demands of schedule
- Decline of energy
- Pain
- Vision loss
- Hearing loss
- Inability to achieve goals
- Perfectionism
- Indecision
- Unnecessary worry
- Upset over minor irritations
- Disorder
- Disorganization
- Procrastination
- Pleasing others
- Anxiety over presentations
- Judgmentalism
- Space shortage
- Aging—"Can't do what I used to"
- Taking on too much responsibility
- Memory loss
- Loneliness
- Uncertainty

Health changes and concerns, the most prominent stressor (12), is followed by caregiver stress (4), loss and grief (4), financial concerns (3), vision loss (3), family crises (2, pain (2), and hearing loss (2). This informal telephone survey is neither exhaustive nor in-depth, but it gives a general idea of some of the stressors seniors experience. No doubt, some of the stressors mentioned have been life-long, such as procrastination, perfectionism, disorder, uncertainty, and disorganization. Those seniors living in a retirement community can greatly reduce, if not eliminate, the stresses of upkeep and maintenance of a home, meal preparations, and security concerns.

The seniors I interviewed seemed able to cope well and to manage their stress. Most of them also recognized that a certain level of stress can be a good thing.

Stress Management

How can one best manage stress and keep it at an acceptable level? The following are a few suggestions for the reduction of your stress.

Identify your stressors. Make a list of the things that are stressful. Note which ones you might be able to eliminate. Avoid stressful situations. Avoid taking on more activities or responsibilities than you can handle. Learn to say no. Say yes to those things that fall within your comfort level. If we have a choice, it may seem wise to handle only one thing at a time. Too many stressors deplete body energy and reserves.

Deep Breathing

Deep, full breaths originating in the abdomen can be very relaxing. This is how to do it: Sit quietly and comfortably in a chair with feet on the floor. (An erect posture is best.) As you inhale, let your abdomen expand. Hold your breath for a few seconds and then slowly exhale. Repeat this breathing cycle ten times and feel the relaxation flowing into your body. The companions of shallow breathing are usually fear, anxiety, and anger, but the companions of deep breathing are calmness, serenity, and peace.

Progressive Relaxation

This involves tensing up a particular muscle system of the body, drawing in a deep breath, holding for a few seconds, and then letting the breath go. One may start with the feet, followed by the calf muscles, thighs, buttocks, abdomen, chest, shoulders, arms and hands, neck, jaw, face, and scalp. One may also tense all muscular systems of the body simultaneously, hold, and then release. If stress tenses up the body, progressive relaxation is an effective tool to release the excess tension.

There are numerous strategies for the management of stress. Exercise, a healthy and balanced diet, massage, communion with nature, conversing with a trusted friend, an enjoyable hobby, inspirational literature, and meditation are just a few of the ways to manage stress.

What role can spirituality play in the alleviation of stress? Spirituality provides a perspective from which to view all of life's events. It informs us that God is present in the midst of all our stresses. In the storms, fierce winds, and powerful waves that threaten to capsize our flimsy vessels, it is the calming voice that whispers, "peace, be still." In my ministry as a hospital chaplain, where I was present with patients and families dealing with the stressors of serious illness, dying, death, loss, and grief, they sought an eternal word, a word from God that would sustain and guide them through their crises. When a patient could say, "I'm in God's hands no matter what happens," I knew a surrender was taking place. In my own hospitalizations and close brushes with death, I came to a place of peace and rest by surrendering myself to God's grace, mercy, and love.

Spirituality is the bridge between earth and heaven. By looking to heaven, rather than being fixated with earthly cares, we will surely discover a perspective that will transcend our stressors. In the midst of being stoned to death, Stephen "gazed into heaven and saw the glory of God and Jesus standing at the right hand of God" (Acts 7:55). Stephen found the bridge from earth to heaven. In so doing, he left behind all earthly stress and strain. In our own way each of us has the opportunity to look for and find that bridge leading to heaven.

CHAPTER 4

Spirituality, Imagination, and Healing

Ever since I can remember, I have had a lively imagination. In grade school I was a "daydreamer." A daydream, for example, could transport me right out of the classroom into a world of beauty, danger, or adventure. I could look at a picture of a Civil War battle and imagine myself there participating in the battle. I could read about the adventures of Huckleberry Finn and imagine myself floating down the Mississippi River. I still haven't forgotten this vision, and in my adventurous heart I would still like to do it. My rich imagination was a source of delight to me, although my sixth grade teacher, Emily Crist, thought I carried it too far. Once when I was involved in a daydream and looking out the window, she cracked my knuckles with her old hickory stick, reminding me that "time waits on no man."

Every Sunday morning I faithfully attended church with my parents and brothers. Not infrequently, as I watched the pastor lead the worship service, deliver a sermon, and greet people at the doorway, I imagined that one day I might like to be a pastor. As I went through high school, a year in the U.S. Navy, and college, I pretty much forgot about my childhood vision. During college I had majored in geology, but because it did not involve enough interaction with people, I turned to a career in high-school teaching. Interestingly enough, my childhood vision hadn't disappeared, for after one year of high-school teaching, I experienced a strong inner conviction to go to seminary and prepare to become a pastor. I followed this inner calling, and in June 1957 I graduated from the North Park Theological Seminary in Chicago, Illinois. I pastored several Covenant Churches and then became a hospital pastor (chaplain); in this field I spent the major part of my career.

The imaginer had become what he had imagined!

Why do some imaginings become reality, while others do not? As we will later discover, it has to do with emotional investment and the frequency and vividness of the imagined vision.

It would appear that imagination is the basis of all that we think, do, and plan. What architect did not first imagine, in his or her mind's eye, the completed project, before drawing the blueprint? What artist did not first dream of his or her picture before painting it? What poet did not first imagine his or her poem before composing it? Recently, I composed a poem entitled "Walking with Death at Midnight." In this poem I imagined myself in an old cemetery on a moonlit night, walking among the gravestones and dialoguing with my loved ones who lay buried there. One person, after reading the poem, asked if I had actually been there. My answer was yes. In my imagination I was actually there!

Imagination is both a transporter and a creator. It can take us wherever we want to go, and once there, it can create whatever reality we want to take place.

Before I married Marguerite, I imagined what it would be like to have her as my wife. I could see us living in our own home, sharing meals, and sitting in a cozy living room with our own furniture. The more I imagined it, the more I could see it taking place. One day I asked her to marry me, and the dream became a reality. Now, almost fifty years later, the dream has been a great blessing, and it still is today.

Imagination and Creation

Does God have an imagination? If this is so, did God use imagination to bring all creation into being?

In Romans 4:17b, we read that God gives life to the dead and calls into being that which does not exist. How does God create out of formlessness, nothingness, and darkness (Gen. 1:2)? "God said, 'Let there be light'; and there was light" (Gen. 1:3). How did this happen?

I propose that it first happened through God's lively and vivid imagination. If this is so, then the birds, fish, plants, trees, and animals were all imagined by God and then called into being. This theory gains even more support when it comes to the creation of man and woman: "So God created humankind in his image, / in the image of God he created them; / male and female he created them" (Gen. 1:27). This passage makes it clear that each human being is created as a divine image. We are the product of the imagination of God. This means that, like God, we have the capacity to create through our imagination. We, too, like God, can call into being that which did not exist. When you use your imagination to call something into being, you are a co-creator with God.

God blessed man and woman and told them to be fruitful and multiply and to fill the earth (Gen. 1:28). Whenever we creatively use our imagination, we are being fruitful and filling the earth with the kind of fruit that will benefit humankind. When we imagine and give birth to peace, we are giving a gift that will enhance all of humankind and will ultimately work for the peace of the nations, who are too often involved in violence.

Unfortunately, imagination can also be used negatively. Negative imagination bears bitter fruit. It can yield hurt, pain, fear, resentment, grief, disease, and violence. Consciously or unconsciously, in one degree or another, most of us have indulged in some form of negative imagination.

What is the price of negative imaginings? It is costly, for it results in unhappiness, disharmony, and nonfulfillment. Therefore, it is well to be aware of our images and to direct them into positive channels.

Trusting and Giving Birth to Imagination

Morning, noon, and night, images may bubble up and present themselves to our consciousness. We may, for example, see an image of ourselves hiking in the mountains, visiting or making a telephone call to a friend, painting a picture, reading a book, or dining with a spouse or friend. Most of these are trustworthy images, and we give birth to many of them on a daily basis. Other images that come our way may be more difficult to trust.

Let us look for a moment at the images in the life of Jesus. He saw himself as a suffering servant. The consequence of this image was severe, for it led him to the anguish of the Garden of Gethsemane and ultimately to death on a cross. However, he also had the triumphant images of an empty tomb and resurrection. Could you imagine yourself as a suffering servant in this day and age? Would this be an image that is difficult to trust? It may not be as far-fetched as you think. If you are willing to give time and effort for the well-being of another person, if you are willing to go the extra mile regardless of personal cost, you may be a modern-day suffering servant. Images are unique, and each person will have a different set of images.

In January 1999, I had an image of myself writing a book. In my mind's eye I imagined the book to be a manual on spirituality for seniors. I could see the book finished and published. I trusted the original image, and I still trust it. However, it is the birthing process that has required hard and disciplined work.

The fact that the birthing of some images may require patience, endurance, hard work, and discipline should not cause us to shy away from them. It is these very images that will provide us the most joy, reward, and satisfaction. I can already anticipate the joy and enormous satisfaction that will be mine once my book is complete. Additionally, the birthing of an image will bolster our confidence and make us ready to trust another image and bring it to completion.

The following comment by Ranier Maria Rilke goes right to the heart of this process involved in giving birth to an image.

> You must give birth to your images. They are the future waiting to be born. Fear not the strangeness you feel. The future must enter into you long before it happens. Just wait for the birth, for the hour of new clarity.[1]

The Source of Imagination

Where do our images come from? It seems safe to say that they do not proceed from the logical or conscious mind. This part of the mind, often referred to as the left hemisphere of the brain, has cognitive abilities and analysis. It processes and organizes information. Images that flow from the unconscious mind are unprocessed, fresh, and untamed. Dreams, which flow out of the unconscious mind, are symbolic images.

Carl Jung was the groundbreaking pioneer in the exploration of the unconscious or subconscious mind. He developed a process that he called "active imagination."[2] It involved having a dialogue with images that would bubble up from the unconscious. For example, Barbara Hannah, a student of Jung's, reported that one of her clients had a fruitful dialogue with a great mother image.[3] For those readers who desire to become more familiar with the technique of active imagination, please consult Barbara Hannah's book *Active Imagination.*

The right hemisphere of the brain is nonlogical and has to do with hunches, intuition, and creativity. It is the part that gives expression to our images and imagination.

While the realities of daily life require that people use both left-brain and right-brain hemispheres, a person will usually be more dominant in one or the other. Artists, for example, may tend to be more right-brained than left-brained, for they draw freely from their intuition and feelings in their creative work.

The more one honors and acts on images that bubble up from the unconscious, the more abundant they will become. Such images can bring color and richness to life and can lead to greater creativity.

After having provided some insights into the origin, character, and importance of imagination, I will now focus on the role of imagination in healing.

Imagination in History

Imagery is one of the world's oldest and greatest healing resources and it has always had a profound affect on health. Images affect the emotions and can trigger changes in biochemistry, blood pressure, brain waves, and blood sugar levels. Images may shape life, and they may also determine death.

Images communicate with tissues and organs, even cells, to effect a change.[4] Humankind has known the power of the image since the dawn of human civilization. It has been expressed in various ways, including rituals, rites, and symbols. During the last decades of the twentieth century, scientific research confirmed the power of the image and heightened our awareness of its intricate workings.

Shamanism

Modern man may be unfamiliar with shamanism and may therefore consider it to be irrelevant and too extreme, having little to do with the contemporary healing scene. If you fit into this category, the following discussion may help toward gaining a better understanding of the nature and practice of shamanism, which is the most widely practiced medicine on the planet today. It is at least twenty thousand years old.

What is the work of the shaman? It involves using vivid images, rituals, rites, symbols, costumes, and music (such as the beating of a drum), and it aims at bringing about a state of harmony and wholeness in an individual. It is first and foremost a path that focuses on spiritual unity with the universe.

The shaman is priest, physician, and exorcist who ascends into the sky or descends into the underworld to gain power and knowledge of what might be required to bring a soul into harmonious relationship with neighbors, God, and creation. It is more important to the shaman to save a soul than to effect a cure, although the latter may take place.

Through various rituals, especially the beating of the drum, the shaman may induce an altered state of consciousness in the patient. In an altered state or a trance, the patient is receptive to change and healing. Additionally, the shaman brings about a heightened state of expectancy, which is an important ingredient in the healing process. The shaman excites, concentrates, and intensifies the imagination of his patient to a point that what has been imagined becomes real.

In his work, the shaman does not try to avoid death. The important thing is for the patient to be aligned with and in harmony with the spirit world. The shaman conducts rites of passage for birth, puberty, marriage, and death. The shaman may use sickness as a vehicle to learn lessons and to reach a higher state of consciousness. The shaman's work bypasses the intellect, or logical mind, to engage the imagination and intuitive part of the mind.

One example of shamanic healing practices comes from the Navaho, a North American Indian tribe. The patient sits in the center of a circle surrounded by tribal members. Sand painting, rattles, and chants induce vivid imagination and a state of expectancy. The healing ceremony may continue for fifty or one hundred hours and may produce a state of hypnosis in which the ailing tribal member may be healed.[5]

In the shaman's work, there is no distinction between body, mind, and spirit. Body is mind, and mind is spirit.

Asclepian Healing Centers

In the fourth century B.C.E. some two hundred Asclepian temples were created and dedicated to Asclepius, the Greek god of medicine. It was believed that Asclepius had not only a vast knowledge of the healing arts but also the power to heal a wide variety of diseases.

Let us imagine that you lived in the year 402 B.C.E., in Athens, and one day decided to go to a temple for the healing of a persistent and chronic headache. As you enter the temple grounds, you are struck by words carved on a magnificent marble wall:

> Pure must be he who enters this fragrant temple. Purity means nothing but to think Holy thoughts.[6]

A nearby theater catches your eye, so you sit down and take in a Greek comedy-tragedy. From there you stop for a relaxing herbal bath followed by a massage.

As you enter the beautiful temple, you hear the sound of soothing music. Priests come to escort you and help prepare you for the healing rituals soon to follow. They point to inscribed testimonies of remarkable healings that have taken place. That evening, dressed in a white gown, you join other patients. As you settle down on your cot, you are in a state of high expectancy. The priest invokes a blessing on all patients, closing with the following words:

> Sleep now, dream now
> Dream the dream of the healing God,
> who will come during the night
> Sleep now, dream now.[7]

As you lie in twilight sleep, you imagine and anticipate a cure. But who is this in a white robe? It must be Asclepius! He is accompanied with a staff and serpents. The snakes lick diseased parts and the eyelids. Priests and priestesses, in white gowns, apply ointments. They move as a group from cot to cot, ministering to all patients. You fall into a state, which is at once bliss and waking dream. Your sleep deepens, and you see Asclepius looking at you with great compassion and loving kindness.

As the morning comes, you are joyfully aware that your head has stopped aching and pounding. Priests come by to listen to dreams and verify healings.

In incubation or twilight sleep, vivid imagination and emotional investment seem to be the keys for healing. Healings come from the inner depths of each person, tapping an innate capacity for health and wholeness.

The Asclepian healing centers were holistic, providing activities and a climate where healing could best be realized. The medical arts that developed in Greece, including the Hippocratic oath, had their roots in the healing temples of Asclepius.

Aristotle and Galen, both prominent Greek physicians, continued the Asclepian tradition. They both understood the power of the image to create health or disease. It was Hippocrates who changed from the mystical to the materialistic. This was the beginning of a trend to separate spirit from body.

In the Middle Ages, a period from 500 to 1300 C.E., wise women practiced the rule of imagination. These workers of miracles intensified the imagination through rituals and incantations. The church opposed these wise women, who were often considered witches. Nevertheless, they carried on their healing work among the common people.

In 1510, physicians bound themselves together in a college of medicine, thus bringing an official end to folk medicine and the use of imagination in healing.

During the Renaissance period a remarkable physician by the name of Paracelsus revived the role of imagination in healing. He believed that man had invisible and visible components.

> The visible is the body and the invisible is the imagination. The imagination is the soul of man and the spirit is the master imagination tool, while the body is the plastic tool, the imagination may produce both disease and cure.[8]

Paracelsus states clearly that invisible imagination, a spiritual tool, has the power to heal the body or to make it sick.

Imagination in Healing

This section will consider the role of imagination in Christian healings, mind-body medicine, and consciousness healing developed by psychologist Lawrence Le Shan.

Christian Healing

In the healing miracles of Jesus, faith plays a major role. But what is faith? In the miracles of Jesus, faith might be looked at as imagination in action. To see how imagination may work, let us consider the healing of the woman suffering from hemorrhages (Mk. 5:25–34). For twelve years physicians treated this woman, only to have her condition getting worse. In her village she had heard talk about Jesus, who purportedly had the power to heal all kinds of sickness and disease. From that time on it seems likely that the woman became preoccupied with a desire to seek out Jesus and find the healing she so earnestly desired. It is only natural to assume that she imagined her healing encounter long before it took place. One day opportunity knocked on her door, for Jesus had come to her village. Despite a large crowd gathered about Jesus, she imagined that if she could only touch his garment, she would be healed. And so it happened. No sooner did she touch his garment than the blood flow stopped, and she knew she was healed of her affliction. Jesus, recognizing that his power had been tapped, called out to inquire who had touched him. With some fear and trembling the woman presented herself. She had nothing to fear, for Jesus told her, "Daughter, your faith has made you well; go in peace, and be healed of your disease" (Mk. 5:34).

In this healing, Jesus identifies faith as the healer. This woman's faith, borne by a vivid imagination and strong emotional desire, plus a heightened expectancy, brought a healing from a long-standing affliction.

It is one thing to have imagination. It is another thing to act on it. The combination of imagination and the courage to act on it brings about faith. This is the kind of faith shown by the woman who was healed of her hemorrhaging.

According to the author of Hebrews, faith is an invisible and creative power that, in concert with the Word of God, created the words (Heb. 11:3). In this understanding, it seems natural to assume that the creative power working in faith is imagination. The eleventh chapter of Hebrews is dedicated to ordinary people who used faith (or imagination in action) to bring about the realization of mighty deeds. For example, Abraham, by faith, ventured out into an unknown territory (Heb. 11:8) so that one day he might become the father of a great nation.

By Abraham's faith, Sarah, well past her childbearing years, conceived and gave birth to a son (Heb. 11:11). The author of Hebrews is convinced that the power of faith, working in ordinary people, can work miracles far beyond our human expectations.

I will now discuss a healing miracle of Jesus involving distance healing. In this type of healing, imagination plays a key role.

In the healing of the centurion's paralyzed servant (Mt. 8:5–13), vivid imagination, on the part of both Jesus and the centurion, likely played a major role. It is my speculation that the centurion kept in his mind's eye a picture of his servant as healthy, active, and normal. He never gave up this vision. While the centurion's vision was clear and powerful, it was not quite powerful enough to bring about the healing he so earnestly desired for his servant. When the centurion heard that Jesus, to whom many healings had been attributed, was in his village, he eagerly sought him out. He strongly believed that if Jesus just said the word, his servant would be healed. What is the word? It is more than a spoken word. It is a word that contains a powerful vision of wellness. At the very hour that Jesus envisioned the servant as well, the healing took place. Jesus attributes the healing to the marvelous faith of the centurion. "Let it be done for you as according to your faith" (Mt. 8:13).

Distance healing, carried by a vivid imagination across the miles, is something all of us can practice. Whenever a loved one, a friend, or even a stranger is ill, we may picture them as well and active. When many together envision an ill person as well and active, a healing may take place.

Mind-Body Medicine

Over the last three decades medicine has given increasing attention to the interrelationship of body, mind, and spirit. This movement, which is sometimes called holistic medicine, is based on the work of body-mind researchers and a collection of case histories that demonstrate the power of the spirit and mind to heal the body.

Integrative medicine, a new movement within medicine, believes in using alternative approaches to healing. In addition to the physical, it also includes psychological and spiritual approaches. Steven Rosencweig, M.D., Director of the Center for Integrative Healing at Thomas Jefferson University Hospital, states that medical students must now learn to explore an inner landscape of illness, suffering, dying, healing, and the higher meaning of life.[9] Up to this point, the medical profession has given only scant attention to areas such as suffering, dying, healing, and the meaning of life. The need to include these areas has come about by the insistence of patients that their total needs be addressed.

It is no secret that the doctor-patient relationship is a source of healing. This comes about when the patient senses that the doctor cares about him or her as a whole person and will take the time to respond to urgent and pertinent questions. Doctors who combine high-tech with high-touch are usually effective healers.

When I had open-heart surgery in 1993, I had the good fortune to have a cardiac-thoracic surgeon who is highly skilled and yet very caring. When he entered my hospital room to check me over, I felt a healing presence that bolstered my own healing process.

I will now turn to a few illustrations of the power of the mind-body connection to heal.

POWER OF SUGGESTION

Norman Cousins' book *The Healing Heart* presents a remarkable story of healing. Dr. Bernard Lown, a cardiologist, had a critically ill patient with a severely damaged heart muscle. All the therapies had been exhausted. One day while making rounds with his staff, Dr. Lown commented that his patient had a "wholesome gallop," which is a sign of a failing heart. Several months later, the patient came for a checkup, in a remarkable state of recovery. He told Dr. Lown that he knew what got him better and exactly when it occurred. "That Thursday morning when you entered with your troops something happened that changed everything. You listened to my heart, you seemed pleased by the findings and announced that I had a 'wholesome gallop.' I reasoned that my heart must have a lot of kick to it and therefore I could not be dying. I knew instantly I would recover."[10] The image conveyed to the patient was that of a horse that still had a lot of kick to it.

Bruno Klopfer tells the poignant story of Mr. Wright, a man sent to a hospital to die. When Mr. Wright heard of Krebiozen, a new wonder cure for cancer, new hope surged within him. The study committee initially turned him down as being too close to death to meet their criteria. Being convinced that Krebiozen was his only hope, he convinced them to let him try the new experimental drug. Klopfer reported, "What a surprise was in store for me. I had left him feeble, gasping for air, completely bedridden. Now he was walking around the ward, chatting happily with the nurses and spreading his message of good cheer to any who would listen. Tests revealed that his tumor masses had melted like snowballs on a hot stove. Mr. Wright left the hospital practically symptom free, and was soon flying his own plane at 12,000 feet with no discomfort."

When Mr. Wright heard conflicting reports about the effectiveness of Krebiozen, his faith waned, and after two months his health worsened and he returned to his original state. Figuring they had nothing to lose, his physician administered a special "double strength" dose—or so they told him. Actually, it was pure water. Again, he returned to health. His second recovery was even more dramatic than his first, and soon he was back flying again. At this time, he was certainly a picture of health.

In two months the American Medical Association announced their findings: "Nationwide tests show Krebiozen to be a worthless drug in the treatment of cancer." Mr. Wright succumbed to death within days of the announcement.[11]

Mr. Wright's case reveals both the positive and negative sides of the power of suggestion. As long as he believed or had faith in Krebiozen, his health flourished, but when his belief and faith waned, he succumbed to his illness.

When authoritative words are taken into the heart, consequences will follow either for good or for ill. Proverbs declares, "As he thinks in his heart, so is he." (Prov. 23:7, NKJV).

SPONTANEOUS REMISSION

Spontaneous remission is the body's ability to heal itself without medical intervention. Eric Peper and Ken Pelliter conducted a computer search using medical library resources and obtained four hundred cases.[12] No doubt many more such cases occur that go unpublished.

What brings about a spontaneous remission? One likely source, cited by Elmer and Alyce Green, was a change of attitude involving hope and positive feelings.[13] Lifestyle changes, dietary changes, and spiritual healing are also pertinent factors. Apparently, anything can work if only you believe in it and passionately desire a healing outcome. Underlying all these factors is the use of one's own unique healing image.

There is a remarkable case of spontaneous remission given by a physical therapist suffering from a massive uterine hemorrhage. She had exhausted all the usual treatments such as hormones and dilation and curettage. The only treatment left was a hysterectomy—an unpleasant option because it would mean childlessness at a young age. She knew that she couldn't continue to bleed profusely without serious consequences. She begged off her surgery for a week and went into seclusion. During this time, she visualized a white light shining its healing rays on her uterus. At the end of a week the bleeding had stopped completely. After five years there was no reoccurrence of the bleeding.[14] What this young lady did not know is that "the white light" has been used as a healing resource for centuries.

For those who will take the time to practice and visualize "white light" healing, it is still available as a healing resource. For those interested in this form of healing, I will elaborate more in a forthcoming section on healing modalities.

One of the components of healing in the case just cited was sheer desperation. This patient, having exhausted all the possibilities offered by conventional medicine, except surgery, turned in desperation to "the white light."

It is good to know about healing options long before we get to a point of sheer desperation. Now, more than ever before, people are turning to alternative forms of medicine for healing. Conventional medicine still has an important role to play. When it cannot help and can perhaps even harm, it is wise to explore other methods of healing.

THE IMMUNE SYSTEM

Keeping the immune system at a high level of functioning is of crucial importance for the maintenance of health. Once the immune system is compromised, we become susceptible to disease. All of us have known people, including doctors and nurses, who work in the midst of contagious disease and yet never get sick. Why is this so?

The answer seems to be that their bodies, for reasons not completely understood, are simply not receptive to whatever germ or virus is involved. It is not the germ, but the turf that matters. If the turf is not receptive, the germ is harmless. In times of colds or flu when all of us are concerned, we should do what we can to keep our immunity at a peak level.

Our immune system is our defense system, and the white blood cells our chief warriors. The white blood cells are always at work warding off all manner of disease that would invade our bodies.

The stress of losing a loved one makes us particularly vulnerable and susceptible to disease and even death. The first year after losing a loved one, especially a spouse, is a most critical time. When a person feels a lack of meaning, has little will to live, or suffers depression, the immune system may shut down, thus inviting disease to take hold.

Have you paid any attention to your unique circumstances at the times you come down with a cold or some disease? I have noticed that my cold or disease is usually preceded by some form of distress or loss. When I developed diabetes some twenty-five years ago, I was undergoing a time of high stress.

Major life transitions such as divorce, retirement, loss of financial stability, and loss of integrity are just a few things that might compromise the immune system.

BOOSTING THE IMMUNE SYSTEM

How can we boost our immune system? How can we assure its functioning at a high level? One of the places to look for an answer is with those who have not only lived a long time, but who also enjoy their lives.

At the center for aging in Athens, Georgia, a group of centenarians were asked to identify the things that contributed to their longevity and enjoyment of life. Five factors were cited:

- Optimism
- No depression
- Acceptance of loss

- Family connection
- Meaning and purpose

These five factors, without doubt, are highly effective immune boosters. They had worked well for the centenarians, and they will work well for all who incorporate them into their lives.

I will comment briefly on only one of the factors, namely, family connection. A family connection in which one feels loved, valued, and esteemed is very life enhancing. In his recent book *Love and Survival,* Dean Ornish, M.D., discusses the scientific basis for the healing power of intimacy. What is interesting about this book is that scientific studies are now showing that loving and intimate relationships result in physical, emotional, and spiritual well-being, including enhanced immunity.[15]

When sickness and infirmity come along, a close family relationship is of supreme importance. I recall an elderly gentleman who faithfully came to visit his infirm and bedridden wife day after day in a convalescent center where she was a resident. Even though his wife had lost the ability to speak, his love for her was unabated. I noticed he would speak to his wife, kiss her, embrace her, hold her hand, and feed her lunch. This was love and intimacy in the midst of adversity, and I was deeply touched.

How does spirituality contribute to an enhanced immune function? First of all, there is the affirmation and self-esteem that comes from a relationship to a loving God. Second, there is support and sustenance, which becomes the daily bread of life. Third, there is infinite forgiveness for the times we have missed the mark and hurt others, hurt ourselves, or failed to heed the cry of a neighbor in distress. Forgiveness is the grace that blots out past failures and gives us a fresh start. Finally, there is reconciliation, which unites us back to God, neighbor, and self. I have found all of these to be of immense help, and because they leave me feeling good, it follows that they are also good for my immune system.

The immune system is greatly enhanced by the power of imagination. When O. Carl and Stephanie Simonton taught cancer patients in their Fort Worth Clinic to imagine their white blood cells destroying cancer cells, they were harnessing the power of imagination. The immune system understands the message of the image. That is why Simonton's imaging technique worked for patients, reducing and in some cases eliminating cancerous tumors. However, in the Simonton program, traditional protocols for the treatment of cancer were not abandoned.

Consciousness Healing

This type of healing is based on an altered state of consciousness. Research psychologist Lawrence Le Shan, in investigating the field of healing, found that as most healers did their healing work, they entered into a different state of consciousness. Le Shan called this altered state the "clairvoyant reality" or "flow-process reality." After training himself over a period of one and one-half years to enter this state, Le Shan began to do healing work. He observed positive physical and psychological changes in many of the persons who received healing.

Because of his success in healing work, Le Shan set up a training program, called the consciousness research and training project, with Joyce Goodrich, Ph.D., as director.[16]

I had the good fortune to enter this program in 1984 and took both the basic and advanced segments. In the training group, we were taught about two types of healing that Le Shan had discovered.

In type 1, the most basic of the two, the healer moves into an altered state of consciousness in which there is a profound feeling of oneness with all things in creation and a knowledge of being. The essential milieu of this state of consciousness was love and caring at an intense and deep level. If one reached this state fully and authentically, even for an instant, the "healee" would sometimes experience biological improvements. In addition, the healer felt better as well. Type 1 healing can be done at a distance or in the presence of the healee. It is important that the healer not attempt to heal, influence, or fix the healee, but to be in the clairvoyant or flow-process state of reality. In other words, the healer does not do the healing, but is simply a channel for whatever healing may occur. At the Le Shan Training Group, we all took turns at being healer and healee, often accompanied by positive physical and psychological changes.

Type 2 healing, commonly called "Laying on of hands," may be accomplished with an ordinary state of consciousness. However, it may also be combined with Type 1 healing. Type 2 is a secondary form of healing, and results are not as long-lasting.

How does one enter into an altered state of consciousness? The use of centering meditations is one important gateway. Centering meditations foster a state of one-pointedness. It takes considerable practice to reach an altered state of consciousness. This is because of the many mental distractions that enter one's mind. One ought not to be upset by the distractions, but gently return to the centering meditation. At first it is advisable to use an audiotape recording. Once a centering meditation is learned, one may then discard the tape recording. Healers may use any variety or methods to become centered; some learn to center very quickly and even instantaneously.

Some of the best results with Type 1 healing have been in working with surgical patients. Such healing, usually done from a distance, may rule out preoperative anxiety and create a sense of peace. Additionally, these patients recover more quickly and with fewer complications.

I will cite an example of Type 1 healing that occurred with a student in an introductory seminar. This student had developed a nonmalignant parotid tumor just below one of her ears. It was quite visible and painful to her. Following a CAT scan and needle biopsy, her surgeon recommended surgery but said it could wait a few months. In the meantime, a group of caring and compassionate students worked on the student. During this time the tumor disappeared![17]

What is the role of the healee? Because the healee has presented himself/herself for healing, it may be assumed that desire, openness, and receptivity, at least on a conscious level, are present. If one is receiving a healing treatment from a distance, it is useful to synchronize time schedules, so that the healing may be most effective. Surgical patients, for example, feel most peaceful at the time a healing group is praying for them.

What happens when one is in an altered state of consciousness? There are four things that distinguish the sensory reality (ordinary consciousness) from the clairvoyant reality (altered state of consciousness).[18]

1. There is a fundamental unity to all things.
2. Time is an illusion.
3. All evil is a mere appearance.
4. There is a better way of gaining information than through the senses.

A fundamental unity of all things means that everything is connected—all is one and one is all. Jesus, who was often in the clairvoyant reality, picked up this idea in his high priestly prayer when he prayed for the oneness of all (Jn. 17:21–22).

In a verse of beautiful poetry, Francis Thompson puts it this way:

All things by immortal power
Near or far
Hiddenly
To each other linked are
For thou can'st not stir a flower without troubling
a star.[19]

The more the mysteries of the universe are probed, the more astronomers and physicists see the interconnectedness of all things. To experience this on a personal level is awesome, deeply satisfying, and self-healing.

Most of us have had a few rapturous moments when time stood still. Once we leave the sensory realm, where all is measured according to clock time, and enter the realm of timelessness (clairvoyant reality), we see everything differently. Everything flows together; the past and the future dissolve into an eternal now.

In the world of the clairvoyant, evil does not have any power. In this realm love and compassion rule out evil. From a theological standpoint this is to say that God, the Grand Designer, built the universe on the principle of love.

There are a few people among us who gain information in a realm beyond the senses. These people have precognitive abilities and can foretell events before they happen. The prophets, Jesus, and some of the apostles, such as Paul, possessed these abilities. One must always beware of those who claim to be precognitive but who turn out to be "false prophets."

In the Le Shan approach to healing, it is obvious that both spirituality and imagination are major components. Spirituality is based on such things as transcendence, awe, reverence, love, compassion, and healing. Imagination is the vehicle that transports us to a realm where we perceive the fundamental unity of all things. I may, for example, imagine that I am one with a giant oak tree, a flower, a sunset, or a mockingbird. In this way, my imagination transports me into a world where all things flow together. In the Le Shan approach, healing is based on experiencing a oneness with all things, including the healee.

Healing Modalities

A healing modality is any practice, treatment, or rite that contributes to the healing of the whole person. The modalities listed here make use of imagination and stimulate the flow of energy. I have selected ten healing modalities, from the many that are available today for consideration and discussion.

1. Relaxation

A state of relaxation is basic for all healing modalities. To achieve a state of relaxation, follow this procedure:

- Seat yourself in a comfortable position or lie down on the floor. After you are comfortably situated, concentrate on your breathing, saying to yourself, "Relax, inhale, exhale, and relax." Do this again and again if you feel any tension or anxiety; feel the tension leave your body as you exhale. If thoughts creep into your mind, encapsulate them in a bubble and let them float away.
- Gently close your eyes; slowly count down from ten to one; and feel yourself becoming more and more relaxed. Let all tension and stress flow out of your body. Let yourself relax to a deeper level than you have ever reached before–ten, nine, eight, seven, six, five, four, three, two, one, and zero.

- Now take a mental trip through your body, identifying any remaining tension or anxiety. Think of these parts as getting very heavy, warm, and sinking down. Begin with both feet, travel upward including calf muscles, thighs, hips, buttocks, abdomen, back, chest, left arm, right arm, shoulders, neck (if sitting do a few gentle neck rolls), jaws, eyes, and scalp. Imagine any muscles that are knotted becoming smooth and warm. See your muscles lengthening and becoming loose. Many of us tend to hold a lot of stress and tightness in our abdomens. Let it dissipate and go free. Let your shoulders drop slightly, letting go of all burdens. Let your jaw drop slightly, freeing it from all tension.

In addition to the above exercises, I have also found it very relaxing to inhale, holding my breath to the count of ten, while at the same time tensing a particular muscle group such as the abdomen. As you slowly exhale, you will find a wave of relaxation sweeping over your abdomen. It is also possible to tense all muscle groups from feet to head simultaneously and let them go as you exhale.

Relaxation is very healing to body, mind, and soul as it allows energy to flow freely. The free flow of energy leaves us in a state of physical, mental, and spiritual well-being. To become proficient at relaxation, practice it every day.

2. Meditation

I began my own meditation practice in the midst of a personal crisis. I was anxious, angry, and threatened by a diagnosis of diabetes, and I needed to find a place of calmness, serenity, and peace within myself. I followed a breath-counting technique recommended by Dr. Herbert Benson in his book *Relaxation Response*.[20] The year was 1976. Now some twenty-five years later I am still meditating. I am still learning and growing in the art of meditation. It has become a safe harbor for me. Over the years it has brought me the calmness, peace, and serenity that I originally sought.

What is meditation? It is learning to think about one thing at a time. This is by no means an easy task! It requires hard work and discipline to achieve a one-pointed state of mind. St. Theresa of Avila remarked that the mind is like an unbridled horse tending to wander where it will. The discipline of meditation is tuning and training the mind to focus on one thing at a time.

When the mind wanders, as it is bound to do, the task of the meditator is to gently and lovingly bring it back to the work of meditation. Meditating on a daily basis will eventually train the mind to focus more and more to the task of meditation.

What are the benefits of meditation? These benefits may vary with each meditator. They may include the following:

- Greater efficiency in everyday living
- Increased ability to concentrate
- Greater self-awareness
- Enhanced spiritual awareness including awe, reverence, and mystery
- A deeper view of reality
- Increased joy, peace, serenity, and ability to express feelings
- Sense of relatedness to people and the universe
- Increased capacity to be human
- Personality strengthening

Lawrence Le Shan, in his book *How to Meditate,* notes two types of meditation: structured and unstructured. A structured meditation contains very precise and explicit direction. Success in doing this type of meditation depends on sticking to directions.

Unstructured meditation consists of selecting and pondering a subject, and regardless of the subject chosen, one asks oneself two questions: What are the facts? How do I feel about these facts?[21] In unstructured meditation, directions are not so precise, but one must stay with the subject being considered.

Whether one is doing a structured or unstructured meditation, it is important to stay with it for a period of two weeks or more. In the beginning it is wise to start off meditating for ten minutes and gradually build meditation time to thirty minutes. Beginning meditators may find it useful to set a timer indicating when a particular time period has been completed.

If possible, meditation should be done on a daily basis. I prefer meditating in the morning. If you like, you may meditate two or three times each day.

STRUCTURED MEDITATIONS

CONTEMPLATION. Take an object—usually an object of nature is best—and focus your attention on it. It could be a seashell, a leaf, a stone, a rosebud, or even a larger object such as a tree. Look at it actively and dynamically. Become one with the object; feel the object nonverbally, as you would a piece of velvet. One may also contemplate religious objects such as angels, cathedrals, a cross, a portrait of Jesus, or the sacred heart of Jesus. Whatever object you select, stay with it for two weeks in periods of ten, fifteen, or twenty minutes.

The purpose of contemplation is to create and carry with us an inner image of the object being contemplated. In my experience I have found this to be a deeply moving spiritual experience. Several months ago I contemplated San Xavier-del Bac, also known as "The White Dove of the Desert." Even today I can close my eyes and recreate an inner image of this beautiful old cathedral.

Contemplation has been used over the centuries by saints, mystics, and ordinary people as a way of drawing close to God.

BREATH COUNTING. After seating yourself comfortably, become aware of your breathing. As you inhale, slowly count forward—one, two, three, four; as you exhale, count backward—four, three, two, one. Soon you will establish a natural rhythm. Take your time. Do not rush this meditation.

This meditation is difficult and requires patience because the mind, as a little child, tends to wander from the path. When you find you have wandered in pursuit of some extraneous thought, gently bring your mind back to the meditation.

Stay with the breath counting meditation for a period of three weeks or more, gradually increasing your meditating time from ten to thirty minutes. After doing this meditation for three weeks, you will know if it is one you would choose to continue. This meditation has many physiological, psychological, and spiritual benefits, such as lowering blood pressure and increasing self-confidence, concentration, and the ability to achieve silences and stillness. In one form or another, I have done breath counting over a period of twenty-five years, and I have found it is worth the hard work and discipline. It has helped me to tune and train my mind and to achieve greater efficiency in my daily life.

REPETITION OF A KEY WORD OR PHRASE. This meditation consists of repeating a word or a phrase over and over and over again. It may be done silently or audibly. Examples of phrases are, "Oh God, come to my aid"; "God is one"; or "God is good." Breathing may be done normally and naturally. The important thing is to stay with the repetition of the phrase. In the process of repetition, the phrase eventually becomes a part of your internal makeup, an inner image of who you are becoming.

In the book *The Way of a Pilgrim*,[22] there is a fascinating story of a wandering Russian pilgrim who committed himself to a daily repetition of the Jesus prayer ("Lord Jesus Christ, have mercy on me"). His spiritual father, a wise old Russian monk, had his eager student recite the prayer twelve thousand times daily. One day, after three months of daily repetitions, the pilgrim found the Jesus prayer repeating itself in the midst of his heart. The prayer had passed from his head and lips into his heart. At this point, the prayer gave him such joy and happiness that his otherwise hard life became easy to bear. The pilgrim's joyful and transformative experience is known as the "prayer of the heart." It came to him as a result of hard work, persistence, and a strong and urgent desire to know how to pray without ceasing.

From time to time, I have worked with the Jesus prayer as a daily meditation. It can be done while taking a daily walk or doing other tasks not requiring mental concentration. It is an excellent spiritual discipline, and if done regularly over a period of time, it might evolve into your prayer of the heart.

UNSTRUCTURED MEDITATIONS

The object of an unstructured meditation is to search for and find an answer to a question. Once you find an answer that seems right for you, do not probe further; simply accept the answer as being true for you. Ponder and turn each of these questions over in your mind. Take your time, and do not rush your meditation.

- How would I be if I were the person I would like to be?

When you come up with a response, ask yourself, "How do I feel about it?" (Follow the same format for each question you ask yourself.)

- How do I love myself?

It is important to face the fact or conclusion you come up with. If your love for yourself is sporadic, lacking, and insufficient, accept it and go on to ask yourself how you feel about your response. Stick to your meditation agenda. Do not probe into how you can improve your love at this time.

- If I were really my best friend, how would I treat myself?
- How is the eye by which God sees me the same eye by which I see God?

This question comes from twelfth-century mystic Meister Eckhart. It is a question that can help us better understand our own spiritual vision and spirituality.

You may want to experiment with making up some of your own questions.

For those interested in pursuing meditation in greater depth, and who desire a greater variety of meditations, I recommend that you look into Lawrence Le Shan's book *How to Meditate.* There are also courses and seminars available on the art of meditation. For those living in Southern Arizona, contact the University of Arizona or Pima Community College.

3. Visualization

Visualization is a precise and specific form of imagination. In visualization, one forms in the mind's eye a picture of a desired object.

When the desired visual image comes into focus, it may be held and directed as needed or desired.

Visualization has been found to be very useful to a wide variety of athletes. If one is a basketball player, one may visualize one's shots going through the hoop. The visualization, in all cases, needs to be rehearsed until the visual image is clear.

If one is a public speaker, one may visualize an enthusiastic reception by the audience. I have done this and have found it to be quite effective. This does not discount the need for adequate and necessary preparation.

The white light is an ancient healing symbol, having been used by many mystical groups. The Rosicrucians was one such group that used the white light to heal illnesses. How does it work?

After creating a visual image of white light, one directs it to the body part or organ that is in need of healing. To be effective, this procedure needs to be repeated over and over again. You may recall from earlier in this chapter how a physical therapist successfully directed the white light to shine its healing rays on her uterus until her hemorrhaging stopped. She shined the white light on her uterus consistently and persistently for a period of one week.

I like to combine the white light with the rays of sunshine. I let the sun's rays enter my eye and visualize it as a powerful and energetic white light. I then direct it to whatever part of my body needs healing.

While in a sitting position and facing the sun, I close my eyes and allow the white light to saturate a particular part of my body for a period of up to a half hour. For protection, I cover my head with a thin white handkerchief. The focusing of the sun's energy as a white light is a very powerful and effective way to do healing work. The sun is the source of all life and energy on earth, and it is a symbol of rebirth. Its healing energy can bring about balance in the body's homoeostatic mechanisms.[23]

I will describe one more visualization technique. Sit in a partially darkened room and light a white candle. Focus your attention on the flame and imagine that it is a holy flame, the flame of the Holy Spirit. Visualize the holy flame coming into your forehead and establishing itself in the middle of your head. See it as a golden white light of God that has come to heal and bless you. Slowly let the holy light expand to fill your head. Visualize it expanding down your neck, shoulders, arms, chest, spine and back, abdomen, buttocks, thighs, calves, and feet. Concentrate the light on areas of tension or malfunctioning organs. Let your entire body bask in the divine golden white light.

Now let the holy light radiate from your body, visualize it filling the room, your family, (near or distant) friends, the ill and infirm, and dying persons. There are no boundaries to the expansion of the divine golden white light. Let it go wherever you will.

This visualization technique enhances both health and spirituality.

Final state visualization is seeing the finished product. If one is temporarily unable to walk, final stage visualization would be to see oneself walking naturally on a sidewalk or path.

Visualization takes us where we want to go, including ocean, mountaintop, or beautiful meadow.

4. Guided Imagery

Guided imagery is usually done in a group setting where a leader guides in the visualization of certain images. (The same process may also take place by listening to a guided imagery on audiocassette.)

Let us assume that you are a member of a small group, and I am leading that group in a guided imagery of a beautiful meadow. After relaxing and being comfortably positioned (either sitting or lying down), close your eyes. Imagine yourself leaving the room, walking across a field, and entering a meadow of plush green grass and abundant wildflowers, yellow, blue, gold, peach, red, and purple. Smell the fresh clean air and the scent of wildflowers. Lie down in the plush green grass and look up to see a clear blue sky with patches of fleecy white clouds.

After drinking in the peace and serenity of the meadow, arise and notice a path leading into a forest. Follow the path and notice the change in your surroundings. Now tall and majestic pine and fir trees cool the air and darken the path. As you travel, the terrain changes. Now the path becomes steeper and rocky. In the distance you see a majestic mountain that beckons you. Even though the trail becomes steep, rugged, and at times hazardous, you aspire to ascend to the summit. On your way you pass over a gurgling mountain stream. Pausing for a moment, you watch the stream as it makes its way down into a lush valley. At last you reach the top of the mountain; the view is stunning and thrilling. As you sit on a large boulder, you feel a deep sense of peace and a close bond of unity with all of creation.

Descending down the mountain trail, through the forest and into the tranquil meadow, you make your way back through the field and to the room where you began your guided imagery trip. Gently and gradually you open your eyes, and slowly become adjusted to your surroundings.

It is interesting and enriching to debrief your guided imagery journey, both sharing and listening to your fellow travelers. Why is it that we like meadows and mountains? Why do they seem to stir our emotions and touch deep places in our souls?

The meadow is a basic symbol that represents a fresh start in life, a new beginning. The meadow symbol is both archetypal and primordial, evoking a deep sense of peace, beauty, and harmony.

The mountain symbolizes spiritual aspiration and elevation. Ascending to the summit of the mountain requires the overcoming of obstacles. Climbing the mountain and reaching the summit is an experience of inward transformation, including a sense of unity with the Grand Designer and Creator of the universe.

5. Therapeutic Touch

The therapeutic touch movement originated with Delores Krieger, RN, Ph.D., professor of nursing at New York University. Nurses who practice this technique do not actually lay their hands on a patient's body. As they pass their hands over a patient, they smooth out the energy field and detect spots of clogged energy, which may indicate a potential physical problem.

Therapeutic Touch, called T.T., is used to calm patients and ease their pains.

In controlled studies, T.T. has been found to increase hemoglobin levels and reduce tension headache pain and anxiety states.[24]

Some 43,000 nurses around the world have trained in the practice of T.T. since the 1970s. On a couple of occasions I have been the recipient of T.T. To me it was relaxing, calming, renewing, and even inspiring. T.T. transmits healing energy from practitioner to patient. Unfortunately, it is still not widely accepted or used by the medical profession.

6. Acupuncture

In the last three decades acupuncture has become accepted as a part of Western medicine. This is especially true in the field of integrative medicine. In 1972, James Reston, a *New York Times* correspondent who was part of the elite press corps attached to President Nixon's visit to China, needed an emergency appendectomy. So impressed was he about the effectiveness of acupuncture to prevent post-surgical pain that he wrote a story for the *Times* from his hospital bed in China. The story made the headlines of the *New York Times,* thus making the public aware of the value of acupuncture.

Acupuncture has been practiced in China for the past three thousand years. It is based on Chi (life energy), which acupuncture needles stimulate. The needles are placed on body meridians, wherever the body needs energy or pain relief.

I have had acupuncture treatments for both pain relief and stimulation of organs such as the liver, kidneys, and heart. The needles are not painful. My acupuncturist, who was trained in China, invited me to lie down and relax on a comfortable table after inserting the needles. He dimmed the lights and left the room. The needles remained in place for thirty to forty minutes. I always came away feeling relaxed and energized.

Acupuncture is now being combined with other therapies including chiropractic. Some insurance carriers fund it, but funding is not yet available through Medicare.

7. Therapeutic Massage

Today, massage is widely available. It is a wonderful way to enhance health and well-being. I am a fan of massage. Over the past fifteen years I have found physical, emotional, and spiritual benefits by receiving massage on a weekly or biweekly basis. One of the most important things for anyone who deals with diabetes is good circulation, especially to the extremities (feet, legs, and hands). Massage has helped me maintain good circulation. Emotionally it has reduced anxiety, and spiritually it has increased a sense of oneness with God, neighbor, and myself. (For me, oneness is enhanced by a state of well-being and relaxation, which massage promotes.)

Massage is an ancient therapy. Records from ancient civilizations show that some form of touching was practiced for therapeutic purposes. The modern form of massage practiced by most Western massage therapists originated in Sweden in the late eighteenth century.

Most human beings love to touch and be touched, but a professionally trained massage therapist knows where and how to apply touch for maximum benefit.

Following are a list of benefits that one may receive from massage.[25]

- Relaxes
- Increases circulation and blood flow
- Relieves pain from and hastens healing of injuries
- Loosens tight muscles, resulting in greater range of motion and flexibility
- Improves detoxifying functions of the lymphatic system
- Strengthens immune system
- Relieves stress
- Keeps skin functioning in a normal, healthy manner
- Calms nervous system
- Promotes overall sense of well-being

When going for a massage, it is important to seek out a qualified therapist. Such therapists will be licensed massage therapists (L.M.T.), indicating they have gone through a school of massage therapy.

8. Confession

Confession is the act of acknowledging one's sins, shortcomings, or wrongdoings to oneself, to another person, or to God. It is the unburdening of one's soul and letting go of buried guilt, resentment, or hostility.

Buried guilt and sin sickens soul and body, but confessed guilt and sin heals and makes soul and body well.

In the apostolic church, confession, forgiveness, and healing were all tied together. James, one of the early apostles, put it this way: "Confess your sins to one another, and pray for one another, that you may be healed" (Jas. 5:16a). John, another early apostle, declared, "If we confess our sins, he who is faithful and just will forgive us our sins and cleanse us from all unrighteousness" (1 Jn. 1:9).

My own personal experience with confession has convinced me that it is healing. Like all human beings, I have committed sins, misbehaved, and in the process hurt others and myself. I have found that when I bury or suppress my sins, I feel miserable and burdened in both body and soul. However, when I confess my sin and get it out into the open, I feel relieved, free, and healed. This is not to say that confession is easy. In fact, it can be difficult and painful. This is especially true when you make confession to a loved one or friend whom you have hurt.

In the Roman Catholic tradition, confession is a sacrament. It had usually been known as the sacrament of penance, but in recent times it has been known as the sacrament of reconciliation, since most confessions have to do with the need for reconciliation.

Another thing to commend in the Roman Catholic tradition is the availability of confession. One can go to confession as needed, and as often as needed. This can be in a veiled confessional booth or, as in the more modern practice, in a face-to-face encounter with a priest. In any case, healing is the result. When it comes to absolution, ultimately it is God, and not the priest or the pastor, who absolves sin.

In the Protestant tradition, confession may be done with a pastor, with trusted friend, or in a small group where intimacy, trust, and confidentiality are assured. In confession, confidentiality is of supreme importance, and it needs to be highly respected.

Confession is the gateway to physical, emotional, and spiritual health and well-being.

9. Healing Prayer

In times of illness, whether it be our own or that of others, we instinctively turn to God as a means of healing. Like the psalmist, we pray that God will heal our diseases (Ps. 103:3). But how does God heal our diseases, and what is our part in the healing?

In the healing of the epileptic boy, Jesus gives us a useful formula (Mk. 9:14–29). Jesus identified belief as the first step in healing prayer. When the father of the boy said, "If you are able to do anything...," Jesus replied, "All things can be done for the one who believes." While Jesus affirmed the amazing power of belief to change anything, the boy's father, realizing he lacked such a belief, cried out, "I believe; help my unbelief!" Most of us can easily identify with the father, for like him, our belief may be incomplete and partial. A heartfelt belief in the efficacy of prayer is the first step toward a healing outcome.

The second step in healing prayer is concentration. This involves retiring to our inner room and closing the door to all outward distractions. In the healing of the epileptic boy, Jesus privately told his disciples that this kind of cure required "prayer and fasting" (Mt. 17:21, NKJV). As anyone knows who has tried to fast, it requires the utmost in concentration and discipline.

A third step in healing prayer is compassion. We need to be filled with compassion for those for whom we pray, as Jesus was. Compassion is our outgoing love and strong emotional desire for the healing of another person. Compassion begins with ourselves. If we do not feel it for ourselves, how can we give it to another? None of us manufactures it on our own. It is the gift of a compassionate God to each one of us.

I see healing prayer as a form of energy. Even as energy from our hands may enhance and heal a plant, so does the energy of our prayers enhance and work toward the healing of another. Healing prayer is as effective across the miles as it is in the actual presence of the one being prayed for.

10. Laying On of Hands

In the healing ministry of Jesus, the laying on of hands was often used to effect a cure. His hands at those times became a conduit for healing energy, a life force, to flow into the recipient.

In this discussion, I will comment on the dynamic and tremendous healing energy that Jesus possessed. As already mentioned earlier in this chapter, a woman with a seemingly incurable hemorrhage was cured when she touched the hem of Jesus' garment (Mk. 5:25–34). The point I wish to make here is that the afflicted woman was healed by a flow of energy. The energy of Jesus knew where to go, and it immediately stopped the woman's hemorrhage.

Jesus taught his followers to use their hands for healing, and it was subsequently practiced by the apostolic church (see Acts 9:17–18 for an example).

The laying on of hands was also used by Jesus and the early church as a means of blessing. Jesus, by touching and laying hands on children (Mk. 10:13–16), gave them loving energy. All of us, or at least most of us, can remember the loving and healing touch of mother or father. The blessing of such touch is something we never outgrow. I have powerful and sweet memories of my mother's touch as she healed me of minor physical hurts and emotional upsets. Her touch and love stands out as one of the greatest blessings of my early years.

Let us take a look at the dynamics of energy healing. First, it detects areas in the body where energy flow is deficient. In a healthy body there is equilibrium between inward and outward energy flow, but in a sick body there is an imbalance or disruption of energy flow. Since the human energy flow extends beyond the skin, Kirlian photography can detect the condition or state of one's energy flow. An abundance of energy flow translates into good health, while a deficiency indicates illness.

The goal of laying on of hands is the restoration of a vital energy flow in areas where there has been a deficiency. What are the factors that make the laying on of hands effective?

First, there needs to be a basic understanding that the practitioner is only a conduit for the flow of a God-given universal energy. No practitioner manufactures his or her own energy. True practitioners are humble and clearly perceive they are but channels of a divine energy flow.

A second factor to consider is wordless and quiet prayer. The purpose of such prayer is to clear one's mind of distracting thoughts and be fully present in the healing encounter.

Intentionality is a very important factor in the healing process. It is the power of the will to heal, and it opens the door for energy to flow into the recipient. A declaration of intent paves the way and is a prelude to healing.

Laying on of hands is effective for the reducing of pain and inducing of relaxation, peace, and contentment. It can be very useful for those who suffer from chronic illnesses and for those at the end of life.

Therapeutic touch, which was discussed earlier in this chapter, and Reiki are modern versions of the laying on of hands. Reiki had its origin in Japan and has been practiced there for centuries. The word *Reiki* means "spirit-energy." The practitioner gently places hands on different parts of the body so that the energy can flow where it is needed. It balances emotional and spiritual energy fields in the body and has a calming and soothing affect. Reiki supports the natural healing system of the body and has been found to be useful in the reduction of pain and stress.

Reiki has been successfully used at Tucson Medical Center by trained volunteers. Patients receiving Reiki have found pain relief, peace, and an overall feeling of well-being. Patients using Reiki have had the prior approval of their physicians. I have observed demonstrations of Reiki treatments in a senior citizen's residence. Even in such brief treatments, residents express feeling of satisfaction.

One form of laying on of hands that all of us may participate in is healing touch. Touch heals. Touch may be expressed through a handshake, a hand on the brow or shoulder, a hug, or simply a hand touching another hand. While making my pastoral rounds one day, an elderly lady asked, "Chaplain, am I still touchable?" I have never forgotten her comment. It was a reminder of many lonely people who need a healing touch. Healing touch may restore a sense of communion with God, neighbor, and self.

Imagination and Seniors

The fall season of life provides a wonderful opportunity for seniors to make use of imagination. It may be a means of enriching, deepening, and bringing excitement and adventure to life.

This process might be called conscious imagination. All of us unconsciously use imagination every day. The idea of conscious imagination is to harness and direct it to a creative and healing outcome.

For example, when I imagine the creation of a poem, a telephone call, or a visit to one in need and follow through on my imaginings, I am using imagination for the benefit of my neighbors as well as myself.

Imagination may also transport one to tranquil meadows, beautiful flower gardens, majestic mountains, and canyons, or to the peaceful setting of an oceanside beach at sunset.

Cultivate imagination as a daily friend and companion. Where will it lead you? That's up to you. There are no limits to the joy, adventure, and excitement of a harnessed and positive imagination. Every day the imaginer may become the imagined!

CHAPTER 5

Spirituality, Loss, and the Grief Process

It is one thing to talk about loss and grief. It is quite a different thing to experience it firsthand.

In 1965 I was invited to Elkhart and Goshen, Indiana, to give a talk on loss and grief. The occasion that brought me there was a series of devastating tornadoes that had swept through their communities, leaving them in a profound state of loss, grief, and despair. At the time I was thirty-seven years old and had been a hospital chaplain for seven years. I made my presentation and called it "Understanding and Handling Our Grief." I was well received and felt that my address and presence had facilitated the mourning process. What I didn't realize at the time was my own lack of personal experience with loss and grief. Now, some thirty-five years later, I have gone through the fiery crucible of loss in a way I could not possibly have imagined then.

In terms of loss, I am a battle-scarred veteran. Most of my losses have been concentrated in the physical area, though not without mental and spiritual correlates. In 1976, at age forty-eight, I was diagnosed with diabetes. This was a major loss to me with many profound ramifications. I lost a carefree lifestyle. I lost independence. I lost freedom to eat when and what I wanted and as much of a particular type of food as I desired. I lost pride in a body I thought to be nearly perfect. Inevitably, I also lost a certain degree of self-esteem.

But there were other physical losses to follow. In 1990, after a cataract operation, I permanently lost the sight of my right eye, and with lowered vision in my left eye, I was classified as legally blind. This loss of vision had many consequences. Most grievous was the loss of my driver's license. An avid reader, I could no longer pick up a newspaper or book without special magnification equipment. Soon I learned that low vision could also lead to dangerous falls and accidents. In 1991, for example, I fell down a flight of steps, fracturing my collarbone and seven ribs. I was lucky to escape with my life! In social situations, I am unable to make out the faces of friends unless they are close.

Another complication of diabetes has been neuropathy. For me, this involves a periodic painful tingling of the nerves in my lower extremities. I have also lost normal nerve functioning and sensations.

There is more to my loss story. In 1997, I began to lose my ability to hear. It soon became evident that I would need hearing aids. Even though the hearing aids helped, I was aware, especially in group situations, that I was missing much of what was being said. In a recent auditory lab test I learned, to my dismay, that my hearing, which was already poor, had declined even more. I am thankful that I can still have one-on-one dialogue with my wife, family, and friends, but I have lost the ability to converse in a group.

There is still one more physical loss to mention, namely, the loss of balance. After being given a very potent antibiotic medication in 1997, I suffered severe damage to my inner ear nerve. While out on a morning walk, about a week after receiving the antibiotic, I found I could no longer keep my balance. Somehow I got home, but I remember having to crawl up the driveway. I took balance training and learned to maintain my balance with the aid of two canes, which I still use today.

With my physical losses has come dependency. I am very fortunate to have an enabling spouse who helps me live a life of quality in spite of my losses! I am learning to accept my losses and am thankful for what I have left!

In my deeper reflective moments I see the gradual waning of certain parts of my body as a prelude to death, or the complete loss of my body. It is entirely natural to grieve the loss of body functions.

In the area of relational losses, I have experienced the loss of several close family members: my sister at a very young age (fourteen), three brothers from midlife to early senior years, my father at age fifty-four and my mother at eighty-nine, and an infant grandson. These have all had an impact on me, in varying ways.

Relational Losses

The most difficult of all losses to seniors is likely to be that of a spouse, a life partner. Being married for fifty, sixty, or sixty-five years and then having this relationship terminated by death is devastating. It is like losing a part of oneself that is now irreplaceable. If two become one, as can happen in a good marriage, then death disrupts and tears apart the oneness, leaving the survivor in a state of bewilderment, confusion, and despair. Sometimes a surviving spouse may feel as if life is no longer worth living. In fact, some prefer to die because it seems inconceivable that life can go on without one's beloved spouse. Familiar routines, such as eating, walking, shopping, or chatting over a cup of coffee, are now gone. Spousal loss is loss in its severest degree.

Loss of a child or children is an unbelievable loss. What parents would ever believe that a child would precede them in death? Logically speaking, parents think they will go before their children. When a child dies, a dream dies–the dream of watching one's offspring develop, grow, and blossom into a unique person. The dream of a vocation and career is lost.

Loss of a sibling is like losing a treasured connection to a common heritage. My brother Ken was just two years older than I, and when he died, I experienced the loss of my longtime companion. We had grown up together, played together, and competed with each other in sports. As we grew up, we went to the same college, belonged to the same fraternity, and owned two cars together. In later years we telephoned each other and met for occasional get-togethers. Now he is gone, and I live with my memories and dreams. Over the seven years Ken has been gone, he has appeared to me in a number of dreams. His memory lingers on, and I think of bygone days that we once shared together. I have lost a link to our common heritage.

Loss of any other relative, such as a grandparent, uncle, aunt, or cousin, can also be profound, depending on the closeness involved. Grandparents can be very special people, especially if one was raised by one or both of them. When my grandfather died, I lost a connection to past history. He had been born in Sweden and came to this country as a young man, settling in Kansas. When he died, I lost the chance to know him better and to learn about his life. I missed his joviality and his stopping by our house in his Model A Ford with a gallon of skim milk.

I lost a cousin in an auto accident. We had grown up together, and I had spent many overnights with him on the farm. We were close. When he died, I felt deprived of a longtime companion. No more visits to his farm, where we had shared many adventures, would be possible.

The death of a parent can be devastating, especially when it seems to occur far too soon. Even when parents die at an advanced age, their loss is keenly felt in many ways. My mother died at age eighty-nine, and I still miss her warm and nurturing presence. She was the "family switchboard," relaying information about siblings and relatives, mainly through letters. Since age seventeen, when I enlisted in the U.S. Navy, her letters followed me, bringing sustenance and encouragement. I bonded closely with my mother and I am grateful that her presence lingers on in memories and dreams.

The loss of friends is also keenly felt. One ninety-three-year-old gentleman recently remarked to me, "At my age, all of my friends are gone." I have heard others in their late eighties or nineties make similar remarks. If you lose a close friend, you lose a valued confidant, someone who understands and accepts you as you are. A true friend may be closer than a family member and may be counted on to lend a listening ear, a warm embrace, and a helping hand. When a close friend moves away or dies, one feels alone and bereft. There is no one with whom you can now share your deepest thoughts, concerns, and feelings. The friendship of David and Jonathan was such that either would have sacrificed his life for the welfare of the other (1 Sam. 19:1–7). Like spouses, true friends are irreplaceable. As one advances in age, the loss of a true friend leaves one standing alone and isolated. It is also a reminder that the sunset of life hastens on.

What about the loss of a pet? Pets, such as dogs, grow to be a part of the family. They partake in family joys and sorrows. They seem to understand when we are sad or happy and respond accordingly. They are our playmates. Many love to chase balls and may also be retrievers. They are wonderful companions, willing to listen and accept us as we are. If family or friends shun us, we can depend on the loyalty and acceptance of our dog. Dogs excel in receiving and giving affection. No wonder that we feel sad and mourn when our dog dies or is put to sleep. We have lost a companion and a source of affection.

I remember the day when my wife and I took our worn-out fifteen-year-old dog to the vet to be put to sleep. It was not an easy decision by any means. Marguerite held her as the vet injected the lethal medicine. One minute Pandy was alive, and the next minute she was dead. We grieved her death and buried her with her blanket and rubber mouse under the towering pine tree in our backyard. Her gravesite was adorned with a simple wooden cross.

Physical Losses

Physical loss is a category that may be accelerated as seniors grow older. The loss of eyesight is a most grievous and difficult loss, because with this loss a number of other losses immediately occur. There is a loss of mobility and independence. Since one may not be able to drive a car or sometimes even walk safely, the ability to get around may be greatly restricted. One may also find a loss in the communication process, because it is harder to make out nonverbal signs. In addition, one may sometimes mistake one person for another.

The ability to read the print of a newspaper, magazine, or book may also be greatly limited. A great help to low-vision people are the different forms of magnification equipment available in today's market. Those with low vision may be tempted to withdraw from life. However, such withdrawal may spawn even more difficult problems, such as isolation, loneliness, and lowered self-esteem.

Dependency is okay. Depending on others for help, without being demanding, will solve a host of problems for low-vision people. Having compassion and care for those with low vision is a vital and needed ministry.

Hearing is an even more common loss than eyesight. The hardest aspect of a hearing loss is the inability to be a full-fledged participant in conversations. This is especially true in a group setting, where many may be talking at the same time. To not understand the message that is being sent or not be able to respond to questions is very frustrating. In my case, I find myself asking my wife, "Now what did he (she) say?" One may also miss what is being said by a speaker in various public gatherings.

Those with hearing loss need to be patient and kind to themselves. It is futile to think of oneself as socially inept or inadequate. Nor is it helpful to withdraw into seclusion or self-pity.

Hearing aids are useful and helpful, but they are not a total answer to hearing loss. Those who live with people who have hearing loss have a challenge. They may be called on to repeat questions or comments. It can also be frustrating when they see that their message is not getting through. Again, compassion, understanding, and patience will be of considerable help in the total communication process.

The loss of the ability to get around without the aid of canes, walker, or wheelchair is another example of the loss of mobility and independence. Persons who have difficulty in ambulating may also be at risk of falling. Falls can be disastrous, involving bruises, cuts, and fractures. I have experienced all of the above. As a result, I have become very careful. A fall is not only painful, it can alter and restrict one's lifestyle for weeks, if not months.

Once again, depending on others is key. One ought not to be too proud to ask for assistance, especially in areas where footing is unstable. In my case, I have found people are more than willing to help, if I will ask. Many times one doesn't have to ask for help. A good Samaritan may show up just when a helping hand is needed.

Loss of a limb, among other things, represents a loss of body image. I have visited with double amputees and single amputees. There is always the mourning of a lost member, of a part that is no more. Some never get over it, but some welcome an artificial limb and get on with life.

It takes a great deal of courage to go through months of physical therapy and learn to walk again. Phantom pain may occur with loss of a limb. Hypnotherapy may bring relief for such pain. Emotional and spiritual support can also be an invaluable resource.

In regard to other health issues reported by seniors, I will comment only on balance difficulties. Regardless of the source, this issue puts seniors at risk of falling. Falls can be disastrous, and the results may include injuries and a variety of fractures. Sometimes hip fractures may be "the straw that breaks the camel's back."

Prevention of falls is a major concern to individuals at risk and to any retirement community. Fortunately, many aids are available such as walkers, wheelchairs, and electric-powered vehicles. A friend of mine counsels me to stay "vertical." I have taken his advice to heart, as I cannot afford another fall.

Mental Losses

In general, any mental loss is a threat because it may mean a deterioration of mental functioning. Questions may arise, such as, What does this mean? Where is it leading me? On the other hand, some losses may be stable and can be accepted without a serious loss of mental functioning.

Loss of memory, and its close companion, forgetfulness, can be frustrating. To be unable to remember where something was put, especially if important, can be annoying. Sometimes memories of the past are more easily recalled than current or recent happenings. For those with memory loss, patience, compassion, and a sense of humor are key factors for internal harmony.

Loss of attention span, which is the inability to stay centered on a subject, may make it difficult to complete a task or project. It might also limit social interaction with others. Attention deficit disorder is a classification given by the mental health field to those who have a short attention span. I am not aware that this term has been applied to seniors.

Loss of control of life means the inability to direct one's own life, or at least certain aspects of it. It implies that decision-making is gone, or at least at a low ebb. Most human beings desire to control and direct their own lives. Not to be able to do this is dehumanizing. Participating in decisions that affect one's own welfare is a key to maintaining some control. Family, friends, and caregivers would do well to take this approach, letting seniors maintain as much control in their lives as safety allows.

Organizational ability basically means the ability to plan. This would include planning one's day, planning work projects, and planning trips and outings, and the like. Such planning gives order and meaning to life.

Those who lack organizational ability may enlist the help of trusted family members, friends, and caregivers.

To lose the ability to think and speak clearly limits one's ability to converse with others, or even to let one's requests and needs be known. Sometimes this may happen after a stroke, or sometimes in relation to a brain tumor. It can be very frustrating for these people to try to get their message across. Understanding, empathy, and patience are all needed by family, friends, and caregivers.

Loss of independence is a severe loss. It means that one can no longer come and go as one desires. Depending on others for things one used to do for oneself is necessary. It is okay to be on the receiving end; after all, there would be no givers if there were no receivers. There are compensations for those who lose independence. It may be a time to develop other talents and interests, which can be very rewarding.

Material Losses

What about material losses, such as the loss of a place, of space, or of cherished objects? All have an effect on seniors.

Moving out of a home where one has lived for several decades can be difficult. When my mother moved out of the home where she had lived for fifty-four years, we said goodbye to a host of cherished memories. It was the home of my boyhood and adolescence. Every room seemed to contain special memories. It is not the building itself that matters. It is the events and relationships that took place that mattered.

A home may be a storehouse of treasured memories. Leaving a home is closing a chapter of one's life. There comes a time when we must move on, but not without saying goodbye to the dwelling place of our memories.

Loss of space is an issue having to do with adjusting to living quarters much smaller than previous accommodations. Now the problem is what to do with objects and possessions, where there is very little, if any, space to put them. This may be a good time to "de-junk," let go, and live with less baggage. As we age, it is good to simplify our lifestyle. As someone has bluntly remarked, "We carried nothing into this life, and it is certain we will carry nothing out!" The last stage of life is not so much about space as it is about living the qualities of love, joy, and peace.

Dwindling finances is an issue for many seniors. The prospect of not being able to meet monthly bills may create anxiety and worry. Some seniors are forced to live very frugally, denying themselves any extras— or even necessities such as prescription drugs. Some hesitate to ask for financial help, even though it might be available. This is understandable since most want to be financially self-sufficient. It is a challenge to live without worry when finances begin to dwindle.

When it comes to parting with loved objects, such as the old rocking chair that belonged to grandma or the grandfather's clock that hung in the hall, we are parting with items that bring back treasured memories. I remember an old dresser. On the top part was a mirror on which I had placed my fraternity insignia and that of Marguerite's sorority. When I sold it just a few years ago, it was like parting with a piece of my past. It is nice to have our treasured objects, not to mention old-time photos, but it is good to not become overly attached, for surely one day we will part from them all.

The automobile can be a source of pleasure. At least it was to me, until I had to give up my driver's license in 1990. No longer can I sit behind the steering wheel and enjoy driving down a scenic road, as I used to do. Not only is it the loss of a pleasurable pastime, but it also represents the loss of independence. For seniors who do not have a spouse that drives, the loss may be even harder to accept.

Spiritual Losses

It has been well documented that the loss of meaning or purpose in life can bring about a decline in health serious enough to bring about dying and death. That everyone needs some meaning for which to live is universally accepted. This meaning will vary with each person. If not known consciously, it is certainly known unconsciously.

The will to live is closely related to having a meaning to live for. Medical doctors realize that the best medical technology will mean nothing if a person lacks the will to live. This phenomenon is commonly called "giving up." All of us have known individuals giving up their desire to go on living. Once an internal decision to give up has been made, the body will shut down, and death will follow. If the will to live is recovered, an individual can chart a course back to health and vitality.

Hope. Who can live without it? When a physician gives a serious diagnosis or a terminal diagnosis, it is very important to leave room for hope. It is literally true that people live on hope. To remove hope is to remove the future. Everyone needs a future, a vision for which to live. This does not change with age. All of us do best when we have a tomorrow to look forward to. What is your hope? Whatever the hope, it is a necessary ingredient of living.

It has been said that the greatest joy on earth is to love and be loved. However, if one feels no love or has no one to love, he or she will lack the nurture and nourishment that sustains all life. It has been demonstrated that infants who are not loved, cuddled, hugged, or embraced will suffer emotionally, mentally, and physically. In fact, they may shrivel up and die. It is not much different with senior adults. Everyone needs to love and be loved.

Let us especially remember those whose sources of love may be drying up. Those who love another are twice blessed. The blessing is not only in the giving but also in the receiving.

A major meaning for many seniors is family connection. No matter how this connection is maintained, through phone calls, letters, or e-mail, it provides a purpose to keep on keeping on. Displaying pictures of grandchildren with obvious pride and delight reveals that seniors are highly invested and, of course, want to stay alive to see their grandchildren develop and grow.

Life is based on trust. We trust others to supply our basic needs on a physical, emotional, mental, and spiritual level. To give up trusting others is to cut off a vital lifeline and retreat into isolation. Sometimes this isolation creates cynicism and suspicion of others. It might also lead to saying that others, including God, do not care. Trusting opens up doors and healthy relationships, while mistrust closes doors and relationships. Occasionally, it is wise to have a healthy skepticism before wholeheartedly trusting another. Trust is based on knowing another over a period of time. From this experience, mutual trustworthiness is developed.

Self-esteem has to do with valuing ourselves as worthwhile human beings. It is the art of loving oneself, in spite of weaknesses and imperfections. Self-esteem gives us confidence to function in the midst of difficult circumstances. It is having belief in and respect for ourselves. The loss of self-esteem is a serious handicap because we are relating to others from a position of inferiority. If we come to regard ourselves as worthless, then living becomes meaningless and empty. Anger, guilt, and depression may be symptoms of a low self-esteem.

Self-esteem is not a constant value. It may vary with daily events and social interactions. Physical problems may influence how we feel about ourselves. Loss of eyesight, hearing, and mobility can lead to a lowered self-esteem. As infirmities increase with aging, it is more challenging to maintain a positive self-esteem.

Spirituality has been an invaluable resource to me in maintaining positive self-esteem. Simply stated, spiritual self-esteem is based on a belief in God's love. If God loves you just as you are, why then shouldn't you love yourself just as you are?

Care for self is much more than personal grooming and appearance. It involves a deep feeling that you are an object worth caring for; therefore, you will do what is necessary to maintain a state of well-being. Physically, you will care for your body with a healthy diet, exercise, and rest. When I am in emotional chaos, I can care for myself by talking with a trusted friend or perhaps by seeing a counselor. When I am at a low ebb spiritually, I might care for myself by seeking the counsel of a pastor.

I can also take time to pray and meditate, all of which will help restore a state of well-being.

Reaching out to care for others is also part of a healthy spirituality. Reaching outside ourselves with acts of kindness and compassion is nourishing to the soul. All of us have unique ways of caring for others. I like to call others and inquire how they are doing. Better yet, I like to make personal, one-on-one visits. Some show their care by assisting others in daily tasks, some by driving neighbors to do errands and keep appointments. Doing for others gives us internal happiness. No matter how limited one is, there is always something to give away, even if it is no more than a smile or a touch. This kind of gift may be just what someone else needs on a particular day. I once visited an elderly lady, pretty much confined to bed, who greeted me with a warm smile. I said, "That's a nice smile you have." She replied: "It's all I have left." To which I rejoined, "Your smile is a wonderful gift to all who enter your room." Giving away a smile was very good medicine for this lady. It was her way of caring for others.

As one grows older, maintaining a quality of life may become a big issue. What is quality of life? Is there a standard to measure what is quality and what is not? Quality of life seems to be a subjective determination. What is quality to one may not be quality to another.

Morrie Schultz, who suffered from a severe case of ALS, maintained a measure of quality of life to the end. He was able to do this by maintaining an interest in and love for people. He took his mind off of his own deteriorating body by dialoging with others.

Perhaps the key to maintaining a measure of quality is to love others and to allow illness to be our teacher. Loving and learning are psycho-spiritual factors that keep a measure of quality alive, even if our bodies become very limited.

Most of us would agree that if one deteriorates into a vegetative state or is kept alive by being on a ventilator, the quality has gone out of life. At this point many of us would opt to die rather than be kept alive. When all quality is gone, we cease to function as human beings.

I believe that every human being has an innate longing to be related to God. It is true that some, such as atheists and agnostics, may deny the existence of a personal deity. Every human being is endowed with free will and is free to make his or her own choice as to being related or unrelated to God.

What happens in the life of one who chooses to enter into a personal relationship with God? The major happening is a sense of God's unconditional love. The love of God means many things. It is grace, mercy, forgiveness, acceptance, peace, and joy. All of these qualities are involved in a personal relationship with God. Being loved by God does not spare us from the fiery crucible of illness, pain, and suffering. In fact, suffering may draw us into a closer walk with God.

One who is related to God will always be on a learning journey. God's offspring have a thirst for knowledge. Even more, they have a thirst for holiness (wholeness). Perhaps most of all, there is a desire to grow in love–that is, the love of God, neighbor, and self. Learning and loving are the major keys in a growing relationship with God.

For me, the journey of learning and loving will go on all the days of my life. I expect that this journey will be greatly intensified and accelerated in the spiritual world of the great beyond.

Worshiping may be done individually and corporately. There are those whose spirituality includes only individual worship, and there are those who do both individual and corporate worship. Worship is the giving of worth to God. It is expressed in various rituals with praise and adoration. Usually, it is accompanied with music and song, prayer, and readings from the Holy Scriptures. There are many components to worship. This is fortunate, because if one cannot attend corporate worship, one can worship in silent contemplation, meditation, and prayer.

The most authentic worship is done "in spirit and truth" (Jn. 4:24). For me, this kind of worship is best done in quietness and solitude. It is declared by the psalmist: "Be still, and know that I am God" (Ps. 46:10).

A Summary of Senior Loss

First, let us consider how seniors react to loss. Seniors can get caught up in a grief process. Some accept it, and others deny it. Some express a full range of feelings, such as sadness, anger, and hostility. Others are stoic and withhold their emotions. Seniors also are in various stages of the grief process. Some have postponed or delayed it, some are just beginning to grieve, some are midway through the process, and still others have completed it. A few have buried their grief.

What is the lesson to be learned? That it is important to face, accept, and work through the pain of our losses. This is done by letting our feelings pour forth, knowing that through this kind of mourning healing will be the eventual outcome.

Grieving is hard work, but the consequences of not grieving far outweigh the pain of going through the valley of grief. Refusal to mourn can lead to emotional isolation and bodily illness.

Loss is a life changer. One of the hardest changes is to become dependent on others. Having been independent and self-sufficient, seniors feel awkward and humiliated at becoming dependent. It is understandable that seniors dislike dependency. However, struggling against it will reap no benefit for the parties concerned. Dependency may be a part of the life cycle as we age and become infirm and limited; it is a likely outcome.

Can one make the change to being on the receiving end? A radical change came into my life when I became "legally blind." This made me very dependent on my spouse. Her eyes became my eyes. Dependency is easier to accept as we learn to give what we can to our caregiver.

Moving is another profound change brought about by loss. This change is usually due to physical limitations and the need for more care. The big question here is, How well do I adjust to change? Will I resist it, or will I learn to be flexible? If we are flexible persons and not rigid, we will learn to adjust much sooner. In fact, we may become grateful and thankful for our new situation.

Some seniors find loss/change as an opportunity for development and growth. These folks create a new lifestyle for themselves. They make new friends and learn new activities.

What is the lesson to be learned from change? It is an opportunity for personal, social, intellectual, and spiritual growth.

How do seniors cope with loss? One of the prominent ways of coping is by keeping busy. This might mean doing for others, engaging in projects, participating in social activities, and keeping the mind occupied. Avoiding grief may be mentally unhealthy. If, on the other hand, keeping busy isn't avoidance of grieving, it then can be seen as a self-nourishing and self-giving activity. There is a natural resistance to doing the hard work of grief. Going through the emotional pain, tears, and anguish of mourning is difficult. In addition, it is not socially acceptable. We do not want to upset others with our pain so we put up a brave front and swallow the pain by talking about things "out there." Keeping busy seems preferable to losing our cool. Fortunately, there are usually a few trusted friends or a clergy person with whom we can share our emotional burden, if only we will seek them out.

Accepting loss is also a major coping strategy for many seniors. They see loss as a part of life. They are willing to take on the painful work of grieving. They do not feel alone, but are able to reach out for the support of family, friends, clergy, church, and sometimes a grief support group.

From personal experience as a leader of a grief support group, this is a wonderful way to facilitate grieving. Members of such a group know they are not alone, nor have they gone crazy. Thus encouraged, they are willing to share their own grief stories. Within the group a climate of acceptance develops, and strong bonding soon emerges.

Accepting loss and grief frees up energies that may have been spent in denying grief. Additionally, it makes us open to life and ready to face whatever crisis comes our way.

How can spirituality help us in dealing with loss? It may help through developing an inner spiritual support system. Such a system becomes an integral part of self-functioning, both consciously or unconsciously, at the time of crisis. Where does an internalized spiritual support system have its origin? For many, it has been in the making since childhood. It is the incorporation of the spiritual nourishment of parents, church or synagogue, and biblical teaching–all of which have encouraged a direct relationship with a benevolent God.

In my own case, I instinctively turn to spirituality at a time of loss. It is a built-in, automatic response that has resulted from all my previous formative spiritual experiences.

The utilization of faith at a time of loss is highly individualistic and unique. Everyone has his or her own spiritual well from which to draw living water. To be effective, it needs to become internalized and automatic. Turning to a chaplain, pastor, or spiritual reading is wise and useful, but it is not nearly as comforting and sustaining as one's own spiritual support system. After all, the midnight hour comes when the soul is alone, without the support of others. At midnight, it is the house built upon the rock that will stand, in spite of the adverse winds and stormy sea.

The main spiritual resource that seniors often turn to in dealing with loss is prayer. Prayer is a major way of nourishing one's own spiritual support system. When we are fearful, anxious, confused, perplexed, sad, or alone, prayer can bring solace, comfort, sustenance, courage. At its best, prayer is two-way communication. It is more than making requests to the Almighty. It is also listening for the still, small voice within the depths of our souls. If we desire guidance at the time of loss, it is most likely to come at times of silence and stillness. The answer to prayer can be discerned through inner feelings, impressions, and intuition.

If God already knows the needs of our hearts, is it necessary for many words to accompany our requests? I think the answer is no. (See Mt. 6:6–8.) Let us cultivate and place more emphasis on wordless prayer, which the mystical branch of the church calls the "prayer of the heart." Verbal prayers may have a place in corporate worship. However, for individual prayer, it may be better to shut the closet door and pray from the inner sanctuary of the soul. There is much more to be learned about the art of inward prayer, but I trust my brief discussion will have opened a door for those wishing to explore the subject in greater depth.

The Grief Process

When King David learned that his son Absalom had been killed in battle, he went into a period of intense mourning. He went into his chambers, covered his face, and with a loud voice cried out: "O my son Absalom, my son, my son Absalom! Would I had died instead of you, O Absalom, my son, my son!" (2 Sam. 18:33b; see also 19:4).

In a powerful and primitive way, David mourned the loss of his son. Typical of parents who have lost a son or a daughter, he would have preferred his own death. Now all of his hopes and dreams for his son were lost, never to be recovered. It did not matter that Absalom had been the leader of an insurrection plot to overthrow him, David's grief still poured forth without abatement.

In his intense mourning, David may serve as a model, reminding that weeping, tears, and screaming are appropriate expressions of grief. In fact, such expressions are beneficial both physically and mentally.

In his second beatitude, Jesus teaches that mourning brings comfort: "Blessed are those who mourn, for they will be comforted" (Mt. 5:4). This comfort is given to those willing to take on the pain of mourning. On the other hand, refusal to mourn may leave one with serious somatic, psychological, and spiritual difficulties. It is obvious that no comfort can be realized when the mourning process is incomplete. Full and complete mourning is the way toward comfort and healing.

Symbols and Mourning

Throughout history, humankind has utilized various symbols in the mourning process. The symbol lets the community know that mourning is going on for an individual, a family, or a nation. Additionally, the symbol may have a deep meaning for those who wear or display it.

When my sister died in April 1934, a purple wreath was hung on the front door of our home. The wreath reminded our neighbors and our community, and anyone passing by, that a death had occurred and that a family was in mourning. I do not know the effect it had on others. It probably evoked feelings of empathy, personal reflections on mortality, and prayer for the bereaved family. For me, the symbol evoked a hushed reverence and feelings of loss and grief for a beloved sister who had left the family circle. The casket, in which my sister was laid out in the parlor of our home, was also a powerful symbol. It spoke to me of a burial, a grave, and a final good-bye. The casket also evoked fear in me, for I did not want to be entombed in a casket and buried under the ground. I was six years old at the time.

Black clothing or a black armband has been used by several cultures to indicate a state of mourning. In 1977, when my wife and I visited Germany, we found that widows customarily dressed in black clothing. How long did they wear the black apparel? For many it was for a lifetime. This custom was probably more characteristic for widows in a rural area than for urban dwellers.

The black armband, not in vogue today, was a symbol of mourning, particularly worn by men. Black is a universal color/symbol indicating that death, loss, and grief has occurred. Black veils, sackcloth and ashes, and rending or tearing of clothes are also symbols of grief.

Is modern culture better off, having done away with old-fashioned symbols of grief? I think not. The old symbols were a sign that grief is real and ongoing–a concept that has been lost to much of modern culture. What is needed today are new mourning symbols to help us all remember to do the hard work of mourning.

The Funeral

The funeral or memorial service is a very important aspect of mourning. It is a time for remembering, corporate grieving, and comforting the bereaved. The music, hymns, scripture selections, and funeral meditation should be designed to instill hope, comfort, and support. Personal and corporate mourning need to be both expressed and encouraged. A time of remembrance, in which aspects of the deceased's life are recalled, can be very meaningful. Family members and those assembled should be invited to participate.

After the funeral and committal service, there is often a time of refreshments and fellowship. Such a gathering can be well used in sharing remembrances of the departed one. All too often, conversations are shifted to talk about almost anything except the deceased. Could this be because we are uncomfortable in addressing death, loss, and grief?

After the funeral, the bereaved family or the bereaved widow is often forgotten, thus becoming isolated with little, if any, outlet for grief. How unfortunate! The beloved community (of a church or synagogue) is the very place to open conversations about loss, grief, dying, and death. Why is this so? The answer may be very simple. The average person feels awkward and doesn't know how to talk about dying, death, loss, and grief.

What can be done to remedy this situation? The religious community, where many people instinctively turn at the time of dying, death, and bereavement, could offer seminars in dying, death, and grief management. These seminars could teach people how to talk about the taboo subjects of dying, death, loss, and grief. At this time, I do not know of many church-sponsored educational death and grief seminars. It seems rather strange that people who desire such instruction must go outside of the church to find it. I strongly urge the church to reclaim its responsibility for death and grief education.

Four Tasks of Grief Work

J. William Worden, in his book *Grief Counseling and Grief Therapy,*[1] points out four important tasks necessary to complete the mourning process. I will make a brief commentary on each task.

Task 1: To Accept the Reality of the Loss

When I received a telephone call early in the morning of June 3, 1981, notifying me that my mother had died, I couldn't believe it. My immediate response was, "Oh, no, no, no!" When the caller, who was my oldest brother, hung up, I pondered what he had said. Was it really true? Could she really be gone? I knew that she had been hospitalized and was eighty-nine years old. Yet somehow I had expected her to recover. My inner dialogue continued with my head saying, yes, she has died, but my heart was not yet ready to accept the reality of her death. My mother and I were closely bonded, and there was a part of me that did not want to let her go.

Perhaps it was fortunate that I had chosen to do my mother's funeral sermon, for this gave me a chance to grieve. My mother had always been there for me, nourishing, nurturing, encouraging, and accepting me without regard to the anxieties and pain I may have caused her. Yes, it was hard to believe that my mother was gone and that I could no more look at her face or receive her letters.

I tried hard, during the delivery of my sermon, to keep the tears back. I am glad I didn't succeed, for this helped my family, the congregation, and me to mourn. After the funeral service and the graveside committal, I felt lighter, as though a burden had been lifted from my shoulders. From this experience I learned that mourning is the pathway toward accepting death and the reality of loss. I still miss my mother and occasionally wish she were back in physical form to share an afternoon cup of coffee.

All of us are unique in the way and time it takes to accept loss. One thing is certain—at some point, the loss must be accepted if our grief wound is to heal.

Task 2: To Feel the Pain of Grief

Harry was a psychiatrist who had come to our grief support group to work through the death of a son who had committed suicide. He had come to his son's apartment one day to find his son sprawled on the floor, having blown out his brains with a pistol shot. In our grief support group Harry was able to give vent to his anger, anguish, agony, sadness, and extreme disappointment over his son's rash act of suicide. Harry sobbed and wept, allowing himself to feel all of the intense pain bottled up within. Characteristically, after venting his pain, Harry would find something to laugh about. The laughter was not a cover-up. It seemed to come as a result of having been able to vent his feelings of intense pain. Over and over again in the course of our group sessions, Harry would give vent to his excruciating pain. Seldom have I met anyone with as deep a grief wound as Harry's, or anyone who was able to face and express pain the way he did. In the course of time and hard work, Harry's grief wound began to heal. Memories of his son would always remain, but the intense pain would be gone.

When we can recall our loved one without emotional pain, then we know that significant healing has taken place.

Task 3: To Adjust to an Environment in Which the Deceased Is Missing

Edith was having great difficulty adjusting to a life without her husband, Fred. They had done everything together. They walked the dog together. They slept in the same bed. They cooked and did dishes together. They went shopping together. They had interesting and stimulating conversations.

Edith could picture Fred sitting in his favorite recliner reading the morning paper. Now Fred was gone, leaving an empty spot everywhere she looked, but especially in her own heart. Tears would come to her eyes as she thought of her absent partner and the things they had done together. She especially missed Fred's hugs and embraces.

One day, one of Edith's girlfriends came by and said, "You know, Edith, it would be good for you to get out of your home and start interacting with others. Would you come to my home for dinner?" Edith accepted the invitation and found that she liked interacting with different people.

This event was a breakthrough for Edith. Gradually, she mingled more and more with old friends and even started making new ones. She would always miss Fred, yet she had come to a place where she was learning to live life without him.

It is not easy for a widow or widower to adjust to life without a beloved spouse. However, the road of social isolation is a dead-end road. One way to enjoy life is to get personally and socially involved in a giving and receiving interaction.

Task 4: To Emotionally Relocate the Deceased and Move On with Life

There is a tendency in all of us, to one degree or another, to hang on to the image of the deceased. One way to keep the image of the deceased alive is to keep a room the same way it was when the deceased lived in it. Hanging on to the image of a deceased loved one can be done in many different ways. It all has to do with the emotional charge or the energy invested in a particular object and the desire to keep on living in some form with the deceased.

To emotionally relocate means to let go of the image of the deceased. In my own perception, I see the deceased as living on another plane. They are living in a spiritual world (heaven) with their own spiritual bodies. Since I believe that learning and loving will continue in the heavenly plane, it is important that they be free of any binding, earthly ties. I emotionally relocate my departed loved ones and friends in the heavenly plane, where they can continue developing and growing. Loving my loved ones and friends means I am willing to let go and let them move on. At the same time, this allows me to get on with my life on the earthly plane.

Spirituality, loss, and the grief process stand in a dynamic and systematic relationship. All have an effect on each other. The spirituality component is that which brings meaning and comfort to those caught up in loss and grief.

Some feelings and physical sensations associated with the grief process are as follows:[2]

FEELINGS

- Numbness, shock, and denial
- Sadness
- Anger, frustration, irritation, and misdirected hostility
- Guilt
- Feeling helpless and out of control
- Loneliness
- Fear
- Relief
- Yearning

PHYSICAL SENSATIONS

- Lack of energy and weakness
- Stomach hollowness, "butterflies," hunger, nausea, and loss of appetite
- Chest or throat pain or tightness, breathlessness
- Shakiness and edginess
- Dry mouth and increased perspiration
- Headache
- Hypersensitivity to noise
- Same physical symptoms as the deceased

Grievers may also have paranormal experiences and a sense of the presence of the deceased. The deceased may also appear in dreams.

Loss and grief impact all our lives. It is important to learn to identify our grief symptoms and work through them toward a healthy resolution.

Spirituality has a vital roll in bringing hope, courage, and comfort. If one can see and feel one's own loss and grief, and can know how to walk through them, then one will have understood the main message of this chapter.

CHAPTER 6

Spirituality and Preparation for the Final Journey

Remember Friend as You Pass By
As You Are Now so Once Was I
As I Am Now So You Must Be
Prepare for Death and Follow Me.[1]

When it comes my turn to die, I look forward to a peaceful death. I want peace with my family, my God, my friends, my world, and myself. But such peace is not automatic. Like most important events or goals of life, the achievement of a peaceful death requires preparation.

Which one of us would think of launching out into life's vocation, career, or profession without a period of preparation? But how many of us think in terms of preparing for life's most challenging event—our own death? How many find themselves unprepared when the angel of death suddenly appears at midnight or midday, and beckons us to come her way?

When is the time to prepare for death? Actually, whether we have been aware of it or not, we have already spent a lifetime in preparation for death. Our physical bodies know it, for over the years, various body parts begin to wear down and we don't have the energy to accomplish what once came to us with ease. Mental preparation for death is something else, and often, especially in a death-denying culture, we ignore the signs of approaching death. There was once a day, only a few decades ago, that death was accepted as a natural part of life. But now many ask, "Does death have anything to give to life?" Indeed, it does.

Knowing that our days are numbered (in fact, we cannot even count on tomorrow) may teach us to make each day count. The brevity of life teaches us that there is not unlimited time to accomplish our life goals and to cherish our loved ones and friends. If you haven't done so, now is the time to embrace death and see it as a friend and teacher!

As my brother Merlyn was dying of cancer in a veteran's hospital in Chicago, he called me to his bedside and made a simple and sincere request. "Say a few words over me when I am gone. Tell them I've lived a rough life, but that I've set my house in order." It was his symbolic way of saying he was prepared to die. Although Merlyn was "good-hearted," his alcoholism inevitably offended others and estranged him from family and friends. Therefore, his impending death created an urgent need in him to be reconciled. Before dying, he sought and found forgiveness and reconciliation with each of his five brothers and his God. I did say a few words over Merlyn when he was gone, but not without the shedding of tears. In fact, at Merlyn's funeral service, it was said that there wasn't a dry eye in the church. He was the prodigal son who had come home and set his house in order. Merlyn spoke to all of us that day on the importance of being prepared to die.

Reminders

Life is full of reminders that death is close by and ever present. What we do with these reminders may be a clue as to how much we can accept death into our own lives.

As a boy living in the small town of Marquette, Kansas, I will always remember the bells of the old Lutheran church. They tolled whenever a member of that flock died. The bells struck a note of awe and wonder in me, so much so that I would stop whatever I was doing and listen intently. One day the bells pealed for Nate Maudun, a next-door neighbor who had always had time for a small boy to tag along as he did his chores. I was sad, and I wondered what had happened to him and where he had gone. Even as a small boy, I thought it might be a good idea to be ready to meet death. The pealing of the bells of the old Lutheran church was a reminder that someday–and I hoped it would be a long way off–the bells would toll for me. John Donne, in an oft-remembered and much quoted line, put it this way: "Never send to know for whom the bell tolls; it tolls for thee."

There is a legend that claims that the bells start ringing, if ever so faintly, at age sixty-three and gain in intensity as the years advance. These inner bells announce that life is winding down and that one day the final bell will usher us into the mystery of death. The chiming of the bells, if one can hear them, is a call to prepare for the final journey.

Close calls are another reminder that death may be close. I had one such call when I was thirty-eight years old. On Labor Day, 1965, I was doing a home remodeling project and was using an old electric drill without a ground wire, when suddenly I became part of a surging electrical current. I had the strength to make only one yell. Fortunately, my wife, who had just come in from out of doors, heard me and came rushing to the basement, where I was working, to turn off the master switch. The doctor who examined me later said I was lucky that the current hadn't interrupted my heart rhythm. Without the quick action of my wife, who just happened to be upstairs, I could easily have made my final journey to eternity.

Close calls, rather than being brushed off or ignored, need to be used as an occasion for reflecting on the meaning of life. Am I ready to go? What unfinished relational business needs to be completed? What has my life been about? For whom or what am I living? By asking these questions, we can begin a preparation that will serve us well as the day approaches for our death.

Illness is another experience that comes to remind us that our bodies will not last forever. When we become ill, one of the first questions raised may be, How serious is this illness? Is it life threatening? These questions can provoke a death anxiety. Some hide and repress the anxiety, not wanting to face it or upset loved ones with the possibility that the illness could contain the seeds of death.

When I was diagnosed with diabetes, more than twenty-five years ago, it brought a dark cloud on the horizon of my life. I perceived it as a threat, something that could shorten my life, if not take it away in a sudden hypoglycemic episode. I have learned to live with the illness, but it has brought me close to the portal of death on more than one occasion.

Can one be thankful for a chronic illness such as diabetes? My answer is a resounding yes. It has taught me to face, accept, and prepare for death. In this sense fate has been good to me. The threat of and anxiety about death are gone, replaced with a feeling of peace and acceptance. Illness is one of those mysterious paradoxes of life. We don't like having it, going through the pain and suffering that often comes with it, yet on the other hand, it can teach many lessons; one of the chief lessons may be that our physical bodies are vulnerable and, in spite of the best medical technology, will one day give way to death.

Perhaps the greatest reminder of mortality is experienced when a spouse, parent, brother, sister, grandparent, cousin, aunt, uncle, or special friend dies. In these deaths we are not mere observers, but participants. We feel these deaths at a heart-and-soul level. A part of us has died, and life will not be the same without the presence of the loved one.

When leading dying and death workshops, I begin by having the participants share death experiences and their responses to each death. Immediately, I can feel a shift from intellectual curiosity to emotional involvement. Going over deaths we have experienced is a good way to begin the process of facing and accepting death in our own lives. As you read these lines, take a moment to review the deaths you have experienced. Do not hurry the process. Take time to feel the way you responded to each death. Are there any changes you would like to make in the way you respond to death?

In observing your own responses, you may gain an insight into the way you will face and accept your own death. There is no perfect response. What matters is that you begin a movement toward facing, accepting, and eventually embracing your own dying and death.

Within my own family of origin I have experienced six deaths, including my father, mother, sister, and three brothers. My sister was the first to die. She had been ill with rheumatic fever for several years prior to her death at age fourteen. I remember her lying on a bed with very swollen legs. One morning I went to her bedside to ask for a piece of chocolate from the Easter bunny, but Lynette was not there. As I stood wondering where she had gone, my mother, with tears in her eyes, told me that Lynette had died during the night. At six-and-a-half years old, I didn't quite understand what death was, but I did feel the emotional impact and loss. In a day or two my sister was brought back to the parlor of our home, resting in an open coffin. This struck in me a deep note of awe and wonder. She was so still, so quiet, so cold and colorless. A photographer came to take pictures; neighbors came by to take a look and give a word of comfort and shake hands. Somehow, I have never quite forgotten the image of Lynette reposing in her coffin. Lynette gave me my first glimpse and image of death. The purple wreath that hung on our front door for two weeks was a reminder to the community that death had come our way. I was aware that death had visited our family, and I was even more aware that I did not want to be so still, cold, and colorless in a coffin, especially with the lid closed over my face. I thought to myself, "How could I ever breathe with the casket lid closed?" Such were the musings of a six-and-a-half-year-old at the death of his sister.

The next death in my family was my father, who died in 1941, at age fifty-four. After three operations in short succession, his body weakened, and pneumonia set in. Sensing that the end might be near, my mother had taken us boys to dad's bedside in a large white frame house, serving as a hospital, in nearby Lindsborg, Kansas. Though very weak, my father charged his sons with these words: "Take good care of your mother"; then he paused and simply said, "I'll see you in heaven." These meaningful words have been forever etched in my memory. My father's words, as I later reflected on them, had several important messages. First was his knowledge of imminent death. He knew his time had come. As far as I could tell, he was accepting his death, even though he did not want to say goodbye to his wife and his six sons. Second, in order to achieve a peaceful death, he wanted to know that his beloved Mabel would be cared for. Third, he had faith in an afterlife. He expected to meet us all one day in heaven. At age thirteen, I was still scared to die. My father's faith in facing and accepting death and his expectation of an afterlife has been a powerful legacy, and over the years it has enabled me to face my death with courage and optimism.

The death of my mother in 1981 involved the breaking of a close bond of love and care. My mother had been there for me all my life. She followed me with her encouragement, prayers, and many letters. I never once felt a note of rejection, but always warm acceptance. With her I could truly say that death may end a life, but not a relationship. Three weeks after she died, I had a vision of her on the telephone, letting me know that she was happy in her new home. From time to time, during the ups and downs of my life, I have felt her presence near me. I also experienced her death as the passing of a generation. This was a powerful reminder that my generation would be next to make the final journey.

Death came very close to home with the deaths of my brothers Elom (1991) and Ken (1993). This was especially true with Ken, just two years older than me. As kids we had played together, shared many boyhood adventures, worked together at different jobs, jointly owned two cars, and were fraternity brothers at Kansas State. What is it like when one's brother dies? For me, there was a deep sense of empathic identification and a reminder that I might be next in line, in my family, to walk through the portals of death.

Do you like to visit old cemeteries? I am drawn to them. I like to walk among the gravestones noting dates of birth and death, admiring the simplicity or ornateness of a stone, reading inscriptions and epitaphs. Whenever I am in my hometown, I make it a point to visit the old Marquette cemetery where my father, mother, sister, and brother lie buried. I pause for a few moments of communion, recalling days gone by, joys, sorrows, and how these loved ones blessed my life. This mystic sweet communion stirs feelings of affection and ongoing love. As I stand in the old cemetery, I reflect on the fact that the years of my life are rapidly passing by and that one day, I know not when, I will surely join the cloud of great witnesses to which they now belong. In late November 1999, I was inspired to write the following poem, which was based on an imaginary visit to the old cemetery.

Walking with Death at Midnight

Ah, death
I have stood near your gate
but not near enough to know of your mysteries.
Your fragrance is bittersweet
Your steady eye gazes upon all
Some return your gaze, if only for an instant,
while most prefer to look away,
living an illusion, pretending you are not there.
At midnight I walk through an old cemetery
moonlight casts a glow over the pine tree,
the gravestones stand before me, some short, some tall,
some simple and some ornate,
No matter,
If some stones record a span of one hundred or ten years
The dead are all woven into a common tapestry that knows
nothing
of fame, fortune, status or pride
Shells lie buried in murky depths
while souls, awakened to a new day,
dance in freedom and delight.
The old cemetery in the moonlight glow casts a spell of awe
and wonder.
Memories, blessed memories, flood my soul
of dear ones with whom I once walked the earthly path.
Ah dear ones, swallowed up by eternity, you are a reminder
that the sunset of my life hastens on,
and soon I will partake in death's mystery.
Ah, death
Standing in the moonlit cemetery has been good for me
Now I see you
you are a friend
Once I feared and dreaded you
Now I await your coming with peace and expectancy
I see that you are a part of my life—a companion
always teaching the preciousness of each life
that every day is a special occasion, and that
a life lived in love knows no ending.
I will hasten on now ere the dawn steal away the lessons
learned
in a midnight walk in the old cemetery.
As I walked away toward the streets of a slumbering village

I felt the presence of an inner divine light.
Suddenly my soul stirred, took heart and was comforted.
Listening intently I heard my soul whisper
This is the Holy One, the ancient of days, who will guide you
into and beyond death.

In the dying and death workshops I have led, I always include a dying-and-death fantasy trip. In this experience the actual dying and death process is simulated, based on phenomena described by near-death experiences.

After doing a few relaxations exercises, participants are asked to close their eyes, and the leader asks that each person use his or her imagination while responding to the following questions:

- What are you dying from?
- What is your age?
- Where are you dying?
- Who is with you? (If anyone)

Next, I take participants through the dying process, including such elements as ebbing away of vital signs, slowing down of breathing, withdrawal from people and sensory awareness, drifting in and out of consciousness until unconsciousness is reached, and then departure of soul from the body. In the afterlife phase of death, the leader suggests the following experiences:

- Sense of being dead
- Peace and painlessness
- Out-of-body experience (at this stage one may look down on one's body, perhaps being worked on by physicians, nurses, and technicians)
- Going through a tunnel
- Meeting people of light, including loved ones
- Meeting the being of Light
- Life review
- Reluctance to return (back to the earth and body)
- Personality transformation

The leader makes sure that each person, when ready, returns to his or her own body. The leader then asks for a time of debriefing. Many get so involved with the experience that they hesitate to return to their physical bodies, preferring the peace and bliss of afterlife. What this dying-and-death fantasy trip accomplishes for most is greater acceptance and less fear of death. To experience a dying-and-death fantasy trip, I recommend a trained leader in a small group setting. The fantasy trip is one of the ways to prepare for one's own death.

One of the most powerful reminders that people have to prepare for death is the funeral or memorial service. Why is this so? Here is what happens to me. Before me lies a stiff, cold form who was alive only a few days ago, perhaps walking around as I am now, enjoying food and fellowship. Though my mind might deny it, my heart says that could be me reposing in that silky coffin pillow. If a fellow human being has died, who am I to think I am immune to death? It is not that I desire death at this time. Far from it! If death has called this person lying before me, is it not inevitable that one day it will call me? The funeral tells me loud and clear that the bell also tolls for me.

As a parish pastor and hospital chaplain, I have presided over dozens of funerals and memorial services, but not once without a realization, at some inner level, that someday, sometime, and somewhere, someone will preside over my funeral service.

The next time you attend a funeral see if you can let your heart admit that the dead one could be you. If you can, then the funeral may become a powerful reminder to prepare for your own death.

The Importance of Preparation

So far I have been discussing the various reminders that may call us to prepare for death. There may be some who feel that death preparation is morbid and who turn instead to the discussion of lighter and more pleasant issues. For others, the subject of death may evoke anxiety and dread.

The avoidance of death or an unwillingness to face and prepare for it may create unconscious fear and free-floating anxiety. Our death-denying culture, with its emphasis on youth and a dependence on sophisticated medical technology to delay and stave off death, is one more factor in why some people ignore death preparation.

Many people come to death unprepared, and death for them may become a confusing and bewildering experience. Our society today lacks rites of passage or a myth that could comfort and guide at the time of death. In medieval times there was a craft of dying that taught people how to prepare for their last days. One of the prominent sayings was "Momento Mori," which meant "remember death." The Egyptian book of the dead as well as the Tibetan book of the dead are manuals with specific instructions on the art of dying well.

In the past three decades we have come a long way toward opening up and educating the general public about death. The publication of Elisabeth Kübler-Ross's book *On Death and Dying* in 1969 was a giant step toward getting death out into the open, as a topic for study and discussion. Kübler-Ross, a psychiatrist, has spent a lifetime speaking, writing, and leading workshops on death and dying. She also was the first to collect case information and call attention to near-death experiences.

Raymond Moody's 1975 book *Life After Life* brought fascinating accounts of near-death experiences (NDEs) to the attention of the public. This book, while discussing afterlife phenomena, also shed light on what it is like to die. Kenneth Ring, in his 1980 book *Life at Death,* was the first to make a scientific study of NDEs. This book again called attention to what happens at death. Since the 1970s numerous articles, TV shows, workshops, and conferences have all brought death before the public eye.

It is one thing to collect facts and information about death, but it is another thing to confront it emotionally.

Essential Preparation

An essential preparation for death goes much deeper than the head. This preparation needs to penetrate the heart: This is where fear and anxiety about death reside and must be dealt with.

What is an essential preparation for death, and what are its benefits? A most essential preparation is to face, accept, and embrace your own death. When death is accepted as part of the life cycle and not viewed as an enemy, then fear and anxiety will be dispelled.

Another very essential preparation for death is to take charge of your own dying and death. In my own case, I desire to die at home and, if necessary, with the assistance of hospice and/or nursing care. I do not want any medical heroics or attempts to prolong my life. I prefer not to die in a hospital with tubes coming out of every orifice of the body. I do not want to be drugged out, but simply kept as comfortable as possible. I would want to die in the presence of my loved ones and receive their support, love, and care, and–to the extent of my ability–give them my love and blessings. This would be a time for saying good-byes before embarking on the final journey.

By taking charge of one's own dying and death, it can become a peak moment of a lifetime. I realize that my own dying and death may not happen as I have planned, for death could be sudden. Whatever happens, making advance plans for the way I want to die is a wise investment toward a peaceful and dignified death.

As Jesus was dying, the last words he uttered as he hung on a cross were, "Father, into your hands I commend my spirit" (Lk. 23:46). This passage illustrates the vibrant and living faith Jesus had at death. This vital faith carried him from the anguish of a painful crucifixion into a beautiful paradise and to his Heavenly Father who awaited him there.

A vital faith perspective, in my view, is another essential preparation for death. How does a vital faith help at the time of death? It gives courage to launch out into the unknown without fear, bewilderment, or confusion, knowing that the everlasting arms of God are there to hold, comfort, embrace, and love us. Such courage and confidence is based on a relationship of trust. Is God trustworthy? Will you, at the point of death, have the confidence to commend your spirit to Him? It is far better not to wait until the last hour, as did one of the thieves who hung on a cross near Jesus (although even his faith was honored with a berth in paradise); now is the time to develop a trust in God's grace and love.

Faith gives us the spiritual eyesight to guide us though death and into paradise. Faith can enable us to experience death as a peak moment.

One way to prepare for the peak moment of death is to practice, each night before falling asleep, the words of Jesus: "Father into your hands I commend my spirit." Since sleep is in some ways like death, you will be making a preparation for the day in which you make your final journey.

It is likely that few of us will approach death without some unfinished relational business. There may be some people we have not fully forgiven, some we have excluded, some with whom we have erected barriers, and some we have not told how beloved they are. Completing relational business with a father, mother, sister, brother, or extended family or friends—perhaps even an enemy—is something I consider an essential preparation for death. It is essential because it paves the way for a peaceful death.

I will share two examples involving the completion of unfinished relational business. The first is about a sixty-six-year-old man dying of terminal cancer. During my visits with this man, I observed that he was agitated and troubled. One day I simply asked what might be troubling him. He shared that he had a son in Colorado with whom he had not spoken in years. Because this was a matter of supreme importance, I suggested he break the ice, call, and invite his son to visit. The son did come, and the long-standing alienation and estrangement melted away through the stages of resentment, anger, tears, forgiveness, holding hands, love, and hugs. Father and son were reconciled to each other, and a relationship of peace was established. Not surprisingly, the father died peacefully three days later.

It has been observed that dying persons may put off death until a particular piece of unfinished business has been completed. In view of impending death, the completion of this business is urgent. Therefore, it behooves those of us who are with the dying to give immediate assistance in the completion of their business so they may die peacefully.

The second example I have to share involves the withholding of love, be it through simple neglect or on purpose. When I was forty years old, I unexpectedly found that I had neglected to let my long-deceased father know of my love for him. It happened in the midst of a brief devotional message I was presenting to seniors assembled for morning chapel at the Covenant Home in Chicago. It was the Advent season, and I was sharing a touching story of a son's gift of love to his father on Christmas Day. Times were hard on the farm, and the boy had no money to buy a present. Then, while still in bed, he thought of a gift. He would get up early Christmas morning, beat his father to the barn, and milk all the cows. When the father got up to go to the barn to milk the cows, he was surprised to find that all the cows had been milked. Suddenly the voice of his son came out of the shadows saying, "Merry Christmas, Dad, I love you." At that moment the two embraced, with the father saying that this was the nicest Christmas gift he had ever received.

This loving encounter touched a deep inner cord within me. Had I ever told my dad, who died when I was thirteen, that I loved him? Now, even now, in the midst of the brief homily, with tears forming in my eyes, I would tell him so. So I softly whispered to myself, "Dad, I love you." Having said this, my heart felt lighter. I went away that morning from that old chapel knowing that something important had happened. Now, I know it was the completion of a piece of unfinished relational business. Did my father get my message of love? The inner communion I experience with my father lets me know that my love has been received. Moreover, I feel his love coming back to me.

If you have unfinished business with a deceased loved one, there is a simple technique, called the empty chair, that is very effective. Let's assume that the person you want in the empty chair is your deceased mother. Close your eyes and let a mental picture form in your mind. Next, begin a conversation, occasionally switching chairs to take the part of your mother. If your mother was dominating and controlling, let her know. It is important to feel what you are saying. If you are angry, let this come out. Both your body and voice should express your pent-up feelings. Recall specific instances when you were angry, upset, frustrated, hurt, or sad. After venting your feelings, see if you are ready to come to a point of forgiveness. If you are, tell your mother that you forgive her and desire to feel close again. At this point you may be overcome with feelings of love. If so, give your mother a hug and tell her you love her. It is a foregone conclusion that mother will reciprocate with love, understanding, and acceptance to you. The empty chair can be done in the context of a trusted small group, preferably with a trained leader. It may also be done by yourself in the privacy of a room in your home. I have used the empty chair technique with many pastors, seminary students, religious sisters, and laypersons to help them complete pieces of unfinished relational business.

After having addressed what I regard as an essential preparation for death, I will now discuss the benefits of preparation. For those who make advance preparations, there are several significant benefits.

Benefits of Preparation

By making an essential preparation for death, the following benefits may occur.

- Enjoying life and living it to the fullest. The energy that we once spent in denying and suppressing death may now be spent in joyous and abundant living.
- Cherishing of loved ones and friends. To cherish another is to let them know today how dear and precious they are, for tomorrow may be too late.
- Living in the present moment. The acceptance of death enables one to concentrate energies into the present moment. Once past failures, mistakes, and shortcomings are forgiven, the past may be put in the past. There is no longer any need to worry, fret, or be anxious about the future, for faith opens up a future beyond death.
- Clarifying the meaning of life. Facing and embracing death gives opportunity to reflect and clarify the meaning for which one has been living. It is also an opportunity to shape the meaning according to your highest virtues. Do I love God, neighbor, and self to the degree to which I am capable?
- Prioritizing values. How much do I value truth, mercy, non-judgmentalism, justice, and peace? How much do I value the materialistic life, power, prestige, status, and being number one? Accepting that one's days are numbered can help us sort out, prioritize, and live by our highest values.
- Wiping away fear. Once death is faced, accepted, and embraced, and we learn to live in the present moment, fear will disappear. There is no need to fear that which we have accepted and made a part of our lives.
- Viewing death as a friend. Traditionally, humankind has viewed death as an enemy. Medical technology, as represented by most practicing physicians, expends much time, great effort, and large sums of money to defeat death, the archenemy. Little thought, if any, seems to be given that death may be a friend coming to bear a weary traveler home. A person with a poorly functioning, worn-out body who is tired of medical treatments to keep her going may welcome death as a friendly and peaceful friend.
- Visioning life beyond. One of the greatest benefits bestowed on those who prepare for death is to see that death is not the end. Indeed, such people have had a vision that life goes on after death. Elisabeth Kübler-Ross, after a lifetime in the study of dying and death, bluntly states that death does not exist.[2] Having a vision, such as the one Kübler-Ross presents, can be a morning star

revealing that death is merely a transition into life in the spirit world.

The Stages of Death

I turn now to a discussion of the three stages of death—namely, the pre-death stage, the death stage, and the after-death stage. Can one prepare for these stages? Helpful preparation may consist of gaining knowledge and awareness of what goes on in each stage, plus learning techniques that can assist in a smoother death transition.

Pre-Death Stage

The more preparation that is made before coming to the pre-death stage, the better. Such preparation can help alleviate the difficulty and struggle involved in going through the pre-death stage.

As one passes through the five movements of the pre-death stage, hope is of vital importance. I am not speaking here of a hope based on sophisticated medical technology to come up with a new drug or surgical technique, but rather hope that is based on trust in a loving, consoling, supporting, and everlasting God. Such hope is twofold, as it encompasses both present and future. This means that God is with me as I struggle through the present moment and in the future as I pass through the gates of death. The Christian church calls the latter "eschatological hope," and Paul termed it the "hope of glory" (Col. 1:27). The author of Hebrews calls hope an "anchor of the soul" (Heb. 6:19). I especially like this latter designation, for an anchor is exactly what is needed when passing through the pre-death stage.

The five movements of the pre-death stage are denial, anger, bargaining, depression, and acceptance. Elisabeth Kübler-Ross, in her 1969 book *On Death and Dying* (New York: Macmillan), first noted these movements. Over the past three decades, these movements have become well known to professionals and even laypersons working in the field of death and dying. These movements apply not only to the dying person but also to many situations of life, such as receiving a citation for speeding from a traffic cop. The movements from denial through acceptance are not necessarily sequential; rather, there is usually a shifting back and forth. For example, a state of depression on one day may shift to anger the next day.

Denial is the reaction most human beings have when informed they have a terminal illness. An inner voice cries out, "No! No! No! It's not true! It can't be me! There must be a mistake!" The strong protests made against a terminal diagnosis are not bad or unnatural. They are nature's anesthesia to shield us from facing the stark reality of death all at once.

I well remember the strong denial that pulsated through me the day I was diagnosed with the chronic disease of diabetes. Such a diagnosis to a trim, well-conditioned jogger was totally unacceptable. Acceptance of such a diagnosis was, to me, a long-term sentence of death. I didn't want it! I wanted nothing to do with it. Denial may be loud or soft, but it amounts to the same thing—namely, locking the door to bar the entrance of death.

Anger comes when there is a realization that a dreaded and deadly diagnosis is not going to go away. Frequently the anger comes out in a "Why me?" question. Why in the whole wide universe have I been singled out to suffer? I am also angry that the plans and dreams of my life have been rudely interrupted and put on hold, perhaps forever. Blame, resentment, and envy—all expressions of anger—are likely to be expressed. I may envy those who are up and about and able to go forward with their plans. I may even shake my fist at God, declaring that he has dealt unfairly with me. Anger is a natural reaction to bad news, and it is a phase most human beings go through to one degree or another.

Bargaining is the attempt to postpone or delay impending death. In exchange for an extension of time, such as finishing a project or being on hand for the arrival of a new grandchild, we might say, "I will give you, God, my undivided love, devotion, and service in a way I have not done before." At this point, bargaining may become like a prayer: "Oh, God, do this for me, and I'll do that for you." Underneath the bargainer's plea is at least a partial admission that death is close by and perhaps inevitable. Bargaining is natural and understandable. It teaches that life is so precious that even a terminal illness does not silence the human plea for one more day, one more month, or one more year.

Depression is the fourth movement that is experienced by a dying person. This phase is occupied with multiple loss and grief: loss of body image, loss of routine, loss of ability and strength to work, loss of mobility, loss of social relationships, loss of family relationships, and most significantly, loss of a beloved spouse. This is a time of nearly unbearable sadness as the realization comes that soon one will depart from loved ones and all that has been familiar. It is preferable that grieving be done in the open, that tears be shed in the midst of loved ones rather than in the silence of a lonely heart. Grief shared in the context of a beloved community can then be therapeutic for all concerned.

Who is the beloved community? For me it is found in the context of a caring family, friends, and church fellowship. At a time of depression and multiple losses, the beloved community may provide the sustenance, comfort, and hope that help one avoid being overwhelmed and crushed.

Acceptance marks the beginning of a period of withdrawal from relationships and the world. It is as though the dying person straddles two worlds, the physical and spiritual, with a foot in each. Primarily, the dying person is drawn to the spiritual world. He or she may have had a vision of loved ones on the other side and feel a call to be reunited.

At this time there is a quiet acceptance of death. There is no more fighting or bargaining. As the body weakens, there is more sleeping and drifting off into another consciousness. Now only one or two close and trusted persons need to be at the bedside. Disturbing sounds and noises should be eliminated. Peaceful surroundings, such as one may have in a home setting, are preferred. Favorite musical selections of the dying person may be comforting and soothing as the dying person accepts his own death. It is most beneficial that the family follow suit. The willingness to let a loved one go is all-important for a smooth death transition.

The Death Stage

What is the death stage? This stage refers to the time when death is considered imminent. It includes the hours and minutes prior to death as well as the death moment. Anya Foos-Graber calls this process "Deathing."[3] The death stage has the potential to greatly enhance and enrich the hours and moments surrounding the final transition.

How can this be done? Preparation is the key. The Boy Scout motto, "Be prepared," calls on each scout to meet whatever circumstance or emergency that presents itself with maximum preparedness.

How prepared are we to meet the death moment? Can this moment become a peaceful, and even joyful, encounter? If the dying are to be reached and touched, they need to be addressed at an in-depth level. Providing experiences for them that evoke positive emotional and spiritual memory associations can be very useful and therapeutic. For example, listening to a harpist playing an old gospel hymn may evoke feelings and memories of being loved and accepted by a mother or father.

The series of experiences to follow may be very useful in helping the dying release themselves into a peaceful death.

Dying well is a team effort. The dying will greatly benefit from the presence of a trusted support person. Such a person may be anyone with whom a close relationship has been formed. For example, as a married man I would prefer my wife to be at my bedside, for no one would understand my needs and desires quite as well as she. Whoever the support person is, it is important that the experience provide for a peaceful death transition. All experiences are best done in cooperation with the dying person.

If the death vigil should turn out to be long and arduous, it is essential to have trusted substitute support persons. With a support person on hand, dying need not be the lonely experience the public anticipates.

The first basic experience that may bring comfort and peace to the dying is presence. What is presence? Presence is more than an embodied support person, and at its most profound level it includes an invisible spiritual presence. Considerable strength, courage, and inspiration come from knowing that God is present. As the psalmist walked through the valley of the shadow of death, he declared, "You are with me" (Ps. 23:4). These four powerful words—"you are with me"—are the very essence of spiritual presence.

Spiritual presence may also be conveyed through the ministry of a chaplain, pastor, or priest. As a hospital chaplain, I quickly learned that many patients saw me as a representative or reminder of God's presence. Sometimes it was not necessary to say a word. My presence as a chaplain said it all.

A support person, just sitting by the bedside without uttering a word, may be felt as a comforting presence. Often, the deepest emotions in life are felt and not spoken.

Touch is an important part of being present. Whether the touch is in the form of a hug, embrace, or hand holding, it reminds the dying that someone is present with love and caring.

Therese Schroder-Sheker tells the story of an old man dying from emphysema in a geriatric facility. She came into his room one day to find him in agony, frightened and unable to breathe. She climbed into his bed, immediately behind him, and held him. She lined up her head and heart behind his and held him in silent prayer. She sang the Gregorian chant, almost inaudibly, into his left ear. The old man began to relax and breathe, and resting in her arms he breathed his last and died peacefully.[4] Schroder-Sheker speculates that the old man had probably not been held or touched in years. As the old man died, she felt a holy silence fill the room.

A second aspect to be experienced on the final journey is listening to and absorbing powerful bits of scripture. Probably one of the best-known and well-loved scripture portions is the Twenty-third Psalm.

More than two decades ago, when I was making rounds in the Swedish Covenant Hospital in Chicago, I stopped by the nurse's station to check on the condition of a terminal cancer patient. I was told that she was comatose and there might not be any point to call on her. This was not unusual behavior on the part of the nurse, for some in the medical profession may believe a comatose patient incapable of response. Undaunted, I went into the room to find the daughter holding the hand of her dying mother. I asked the daughter if she would like me to whisper the Twenty-third Psalm into her mother's ear. The daughter gladly agreed. As I got to the part of the Psalm that talks about walking through the valley of the shadow of death without fear of evil—and was repeating "you are with me"—the comatose mother opened her eyes, smiled, and drew her last breath. This is but one of many illustrations that demonstrate the power of scripture to release a soul from a weary body and let it be about its final journey. In the aftermath of this lady's departure, the daughter and I were both amazed and blessed.

In my use of scripture with the dying, I have found it best to use short and pertinent verses, such as "The Eternal God is your refuge, and underneath are the everlasting arms" (Deut. 33:27, NKJV). In this case, the idea is to leave a comforting image of resting securely in God's everlasting arms. A brief verse with a powerful word picture, whispered into the ear of a dying person, is more likely to be assimilated into the heart than several verses. Committing several brief verses of scripture to memory allows for a personal and unencumbered delivery of a timely and inspired word.

Why is the experience of scripture so vital and important? It is because it can be the bridge for ushering one into the presence of God. Such an experience may be especially comforting and inspiring at the hour of death. Each time I use scripture, it is my hope that the written word of God becomes linked up with the living Word of God (Jn. 1:1).

It has been said that music is the bridge between life and death. Music can bring remarkable peace and calm to those who, at death's door, are frightened, restless, and agitated. What kind of music would you like at the hour of death? Answers to this may range from gospel hymns to classical music. Music associated with our formative years can touch our hearts and bring great comfort, peace, and joy. As a boy, I can remember standing between my father and mother singing "Children of the Heavenly Father." My uncle would sometimes sing "The Holy City" at morning worship in our small covenant church. I associate these sacred songs with security, hope, and love. If these were to be played at the hour of my death, I would be fortified with a longtime pleasant association. Since that time I have also been lifted up and inspired by selections from Bach, Beethoven, Handel, and Mozart. I have come to like a variety of music. For me, music must speak to my soul and spirit. This is the kind of music that would help me walk, or shall I say fly, over the bridge between earth and heaven.

During the last year of his life, Mozart, even though seriously ill, composed a requiem. His weakened condition forced him to take to bed. On the last evening of his life, friends gathered at his bedside to sing the requiem. Hearing this music, Mozart awoke and began to sing the alto part, puffing out his cheeks to imitate the trumpets. "Here is my death song," he said, invigorated by the music. "I must not leave it incomplete."[5] Just after midnight Mozart died, surrounded by friends and music he loved. He died at the young age of thirty-five, but the music he composed continues to live on as a rich legacy to humankind.

The use of music therapy in nursing homes and hospitals needs much encouragement and development. Hospice care makes extensive and effective use of a variety of musical forms. Hospice in the Valley, of Phoenix, Arizona, has a chaplain harpist who blesses the dying with her soothing and peaceful music. The harp may be unexcelled for harmonizing and relaxing the body and mind.

Karen Quincy, a hospice nurse,[6] was caring for Grace, eighty-seven years old and terminally ill with Alzheimer's disease. Grace had become highly agitated and fearful. In addition, she was breathing very rapidly. When Karen played a cassette recording of "Swing Low, Sweet Chariot" and held Grace's hand, a wonderful change took place. Grace's body relaxed, and drawing in a peaceful breath, her breath gently stopped. The sweet chariot came for Grace and carried her gently home. African American spirituals, born from a people who knew hardship, calamity, and death, speak deeply to us on an emotional and spiritual level. It is hard to overestimate the value of music to soothe a soul that is homeward bound.

Esther, in her upper eighties, is an example of a lady who died with the melodious voices of her four daughters gently sounding in her ears. I stood and watched the heart monitor waves gradually flatten out while her daughters sang all the stanzas of "Children of the Heavenly Father." In dying, Esther's face reflected peace and contentment. The love of her daughters and their gift of song made Esther's homecoming a beautiful experience.

At the hour of death, all of us may experience the music that is just right for us. The key is advance preparation.

Deep and slow abdominal breathing is a technique that bestows wonderful benefits at the time of death. It calms anxiety, dispels fear, and quiets the mind. One may avoid rapid breathing by practicing deep breathing well before the death moment. It is well known that rapid and shallow breathing is associated with anxiety and tension.

By inhaling from the diaphragm to the count of four and exhaling to the same number, relaxation and peace of mind will follow. At this time, a support person breathing with a dying person, keeping deep breathing on track, is most useful. Such breathing also forms a bond of identification. The support person can best serve the dying by continuing tandem breathing, through unconsciousness, up to the death moment.

Closely related to breathing are sound and intonation. Use of the voice to make certain sounds and tones has a remarkably calming effect on the body. Let us take a look at some sounds and tones. As we go through each sound, try it out for five minutes. When practicing, let the sound vibrate through your body and feel its effect.

1. "Ahh"–this sound brings relaxation and relief from stress; it quiets the mind and dispels fear.
2. "Oh and Om" use the richest of all vowel sounds. This sound can change skin temperature, muscle tensions, brain waves, and heart rhythms.
3. Humming or the "mmm" sound is a quiet form of toning. It calms the mind and relaxes the body. Spend five minutes humming any tune that appeals to you, and feel the calming effect on body and mind.
4. Gregorian chant–this chant originated with Pope Gregory in the sixth century. The Pope felt the chant to be of divine origin. Monks have chanted it for centuries. The chanting can bring profound relaxation and peace. Experiment with chanting alleluia (al-le-lu-ia) for five minutes.[7]

What relevance does intonation have for the dying? The calming, soothing, relaxing effect on body and mind can all work toward a peaceful death. The various tones and sounds should, of course, be practiced before the death moment.

One of the most important of all encounters at the time of death is the experience of meeting the light. Light is the very essence of life. Being filled with light means being filled with life. Light gives us vision, joy, and hope. We tend to shun darkness, for it is associated with gloom, sadness, and hopelessness. Going through the dark night of the soul can be a dreaded experience. The presence of light shining on the soul is a most welcome relief.

Let us now look at a biblical perspective on light. God is seen as a being of light. For example, the psalmist declares, "Even the darkness is not dark to you [God]; / the night is as bright as the day" (Ps. 139:12). A New Testament passage that brings out the same theme is 1 John 1:5a: "God is light and in him there is no darkness at all." Jesus saw himself to be the light of the world (Jn. 8:12), and additionally he charged his followers to let their light shine before men (Mt. 5:16). The scriptures abound with passages that identify God or Jesus as light. There are also passages in which the disciples or apostles have experienced divine light. For example, Saul (who later became Paul) encountered the light of heaven on the road to Damascus (Acts 9:3). For the apostles, being in the presence of divine light was both an awesome and transforming experience.

How does one prepare to meet the light? If it is true that divine light surrounds us and is in our midst, then the more we are open to this light, the more we will be illuminated by it. Spiritual illumination comes as we practice the three-dimensional love that is love of God, neighbor, and self. Sometimes divine light can be seen in an inner glow, a radiance, and a twinkle in the eyes. All of us have met people who are alive with the light of enthusiasm. In this life, people who have some measure of acquaintance with the light will be more ready to meet it at the hour of death.

Another way of preparing is through imagination. On winter mornings in southern Arizona, sitting in the sun for a few minutes can be a pleasant experience. With my eyes closed and facing the sun, I imagine that divine light flooding my soul. As the light streams into me, I invite it into all parts of my body, from head to toe. My imaginary encounter with divine light leaves me with a feeling of physical, mental, and spiritual well-being. The power of imagination appears to be unlimited. Through it we can light an inner lamp that will place us in close proximity with the Great Light that is God. When the Great Light comes for us at the hour of death, we will recognize it as the source of our own inner light. This encounter will be a time of indescribable bliss, peace, and joy.

It is exceedingly important to keep our imagination alive, as it is a tool for putting us in touch with the Great Light.

A woman once shared with me a touching story of how her mother encountered the light at the time of death. Her mother had been in the process of dying for some months and had grown weak and disabled waiting for death to come. Finally, at two o'clock one morning, her great moment arrived. Two radiant angels appeared, clad in dazzling white robes, and came to call for her. As the angels escorted the mother out of the bedroom, she exclaimed, "I finally made it." For this elderly lady, the divine light came in the form of two radiant angels.[8] None of us knows just how the light will come for us. The important point is to be ready and even anticipating the arrival of Divine Light.

Sometimes it is useful to have a support person at the bedside. Such a person can encourage the dying one to go for the light. This word whispered into the ear can provide both comfort and timely guidance.

After-Death Stage

We are ready now to discuss the after-death stage. First of all, it may be useful to discuss what happens immediately after death. The Bible, Plato, the Tibetan Book of the Dead, Emanuel Swedenborg, and near-death experiencers suggest that after death we exist in a spiritual body. Sometimes this is called an incorporeal body, a shining body, or a heavenly body. The characteristics of this new body are very different from the physical body. It is telepathic (can communicate by thought transfer) and is not limited by time or space. This body can go through dense material objects, such as a rock or a building. Jesus demonstrated this characteristic to his disciples in a post-resurrection appearance. The disciples were sitting behind closed doors, and suddenly Jesus appeared in their midst (Jn. 20:26). The spiritual body is also timeless and ageless. It lives in the "eternal now."

After death, it may take some time for the one who has died to realize he or she is dead. With mental faculties and memory still intact, along with hearing and sight, the realization that death has occurred may not be apparent. It may not be until the spiritual body looks down on the physical body that the dead person may say, "I must be dead, for that is my body."

From this brief sketch of what may happen after death, some implications for after-death care may be drawn. After-death care should include the following:

- Respect for the body. The body should be gently and reverently handled. If it has been the dwelling place of the spirit, or as Paul says, "God's temple" (1 Cor. 3:16), surely it follows that a dead body deserves respect. Part of this respect also comes from the supposition that a living spiritual body may be in the immediate vicinity. From these considerations, I have determined not to disturb my body with embalming or an autopsy. This is a strictly personal point of view, and I do not urge others to adopt it. *I urge you to consider your own plans for your body after death.*
- Positive thoughts. Assuming that the dead hear, it follows that our conversations and thoughts about them should convey love, understanding, and respect. Certainly, negative thoughts or put-downs need to be avoided. Just like a living person, the dead are sensitive to unkind thoughts and words.

Because the human eye is not able to see the spirit body of the dead, one assumes that it is not present. Near-death experiencers, in their out-of-body state, provide many accounts of both seeing and hearing what is happening around them. Some who have left their bodies during a surgical operation have accurately reported conversations and descriptions of the medical personnel attending them.

Having unconditional positive regard for the dead is not a problem if loving relationships have preceded death. A rule of thumb might be to treat the dead as you would the living. After all, there is only a veil that separates us. The author of Hebrews had that same thought when he said, "We are surrounded by so great a cloud of witnesses" (Heb. 12:1a).

As in the pre-death and death stages, the after-death stage can also benefit from advance preparation. Having knowledge of what may happen after death will benefit those who survive as well as those who die.

My goal in this chapter has been to sharpen awareness of ever-present death, to face it, to accept it, and to make appropriate preparations. I have called attention to the many reminders of death in our midst and have suggested concrete ways of preparation.

I have divided the dying and death experiences into three stages—pre-death, at death, and after-death—and have presented commentary on what happens and how to walk through each stage. My hope is that those who read these lines will not be caught unprepared for death, but will work toward a peaceful death experience.

Perhaps all of us can come to see death as a part of life and a time of fulfillment and harvesting of the values for which we have lived.

CHAPTER 7

Spirituality, Transformation, and Afterlife

The central question of this chapter will be, "If mortals die, will they live again?" (Job 14:14). Over the centuries humankind has pondered this question. It may well be the most important question of a lifetime. Whether we believe there is no life after death or we believe there is a life after death, this question will certainly have a profound influence on the way we live in this physical and material realm.

Many will give thought to the question on a head (intellectual) level, but how many will respond on a heart (emotional) level? There is a profound difference between a head and a heart response; the latter response will usually be invested with feeling, zest, and even enthusiasm, while the former may be factual, logical, and devoid of any feeling. Most of us end up with a combination of head and heart. In this position we can appreciate both the objective and subjective evidence for an afterlife.

As I grow older and experience more physical limitations, my investment in the afterlife grows stronger and stronger. On those days when I am tired and weary and my limitations are screaming out, I then feel it would be far better to be in my spiritual body experiencing the wonder and mystery of afterlife.

In this chapter we will discuss the various evidences of an afterlife, such as deathbed visions, near-death experiences (NDEs), after-death communications (ADCs), immortality, resurrection, poetry, mysticism, and separation of body and spirit.

What is an evidence? An evidence is a witness that attests to the authenticity of an event or happening. It is an eyewitness account that makes plain or apparent the existence of external signs. The evidences examined in this discussion are based on such accounts of firsthand observations.

How do some people come to have a certainty about life after death? They have taken a leap of faith, and their faith has convinced them of the reality of that which they believe.

Before looking at the evidences for postmortem survival, let us consider the meaning of "transformation." To be transformed means to undergo a change in form or appearance. A classic example of transformation occurred when Jesus took Peter, James, and John to be with him on a high mountain. A most unusual and unforgettable experience happened as the three disciples were there with Jesus. Jesus "was transfigured before them, and his face shown like the sun, and his clothes became dazzling white" (Mt. 17:2).

Another New Testament passage also speaks of a profound transformation that is to come. Paul triumphantly states that Jesus Christ will transform the body of our humble state into conformity with the body of his glory by the execution of the power he has, even to subject all things to himself (Phil. 3:21).

As we further consider the meaning of transformation, it becomes clear that it is the bridge between the physical and spiritual worlds. It is my assumption that every person has a double body–that is, a physical and a spiritual body. Transformation is the process that moves us from one body to the other.

The transformation experience may happen very quickly: "In a moment, in the twinkling of an eye, at the last trumpet...the dead will be raised imperishable, and we will be changed" (1 Cor. 15:52).

All the evidences for afterlife that follow will in one degree or another partake of the transformation process. It is transformation that gives us the vision to see into the spiritual world and behold radiant white-robed angels, deceased loved ones, and friends who have passed to the other side.

Deathbed Visions

Deathbed visions are the paranormal experiences of the dying and the visions they have at the hour of death. Typically, the dying see deceased loved ones and friends, religious figures, and environments of incomparable beauty. Such visions are transforming experiences and bring about peace, joy, and serenity to the dying.

Deathbed visions have always been with us and can be found in biographies and literature of all ages. In spite of the widespread availability of deathbed reports, no scientific study was made until Karlis Osis and Erlandur Haraldsson did such a study in 1977 and published it in a volume called *At the Hour of Death.*[1] This study was based on more than one thousand deathbed observations reported by physicians and nurses who were with dying patients at the hour of their deaths. I am indebted to Osis and Haraldsson for the deathbed visions that will be shared in this section.

As far as my own experience with deathbed visions is concerned, I have noticed smiles come across the faces of the dying. At the time of death, I have sensed peace and serenity and have felt I was standing on holy ground.

Dr. Barrett, an obstetrical physician, reported one of the most touching and moving deathbed visions I have come across. She was attending a young mother who was dying, even though her baby was doing well.

> Suddenly, she looked eagerly to one part of the room. A radiant smile illuminated her whole countenance. "Oh, lovely, lovely," she said. I asked, "What is lovely?" "What I see," she replied, in low intense-like tones.
>
> "What do you see?" "A lovely brightness and wonderful things." Then she exclaimed, with a joyous cry, "Why, it's Father. He is so glad I'm coming! He is so glad. It would be perfect if only my husband would come too."
>
> Her baby was brought for her to see. She looked at it with interest, and then said, "Do you think I ought to stay for baby's sake?" Then turning toward her vision again, she said, "I can't. I can't stay. If you would see what I see, you would know I can't stay."
>
> Then she turned to her husband and said, "You won't let baby go to anyone who won't love him, will you?" Then she gently pushed her baby to one side, and said, "Let me see the light again."[2]

This young mother had seen something so real and valuable to her that she was willing to give up her own life for it.

A typical deathbed vision case is that related by a seventy-year-old widow. She had seen her deceased husband several times. She then predicted her own death. Her husband had appeared in the window and motioned her to come out of the house. Her daughter and other relatives were present when she laid out her own burial clothes. She then lay down to take a nap and died about one hour later. She was calm and wanted to die. Her doctor was greatly surprised by her sudden death, for there were no medical reasons for her sudden departure.[3]

What is the mission of the deceased's loved ones who come for the dying? It is to take them away to a heavenly abode. Deceased relatives are escorts who joyously welcome the dying loved ones to their new abode.

Some dying patients have extended conversations with a deceased loved one. A mother, for example, inquired of her son how he had died in World War II.

A woman, aged sixty and dying of cancer, had this conversation with her deceased husband. In a very soft voice and with a smile on her face, she told him how much she loved him, how much she missed him, and how she knew she would soon join him. She said, "It won't be long now before I am with you." Reaching out as if she felt his hand, she said, "You look well, and well cared for." A nurse reported that all wrinkles left her face, and she appeared as a saint.[4]

Bargaining can be a part of conversation with deceased relatives. A woman, sixty, struck a bargain with her deceased husband. He called to her and wanted her to come. She told him she wasn't ready to go until a particular task was completed. When the task was done, she said, "Now, I am ready to go. I am coming." A nurse reported that this patient died within twenty-four hours.[5]

Some factors that may affect deathbed visions are as follows:

- Clarity of consciousness
- Belief in life after death
- Belief in another world
- Medical sedation
- Mental status

A patient in her fifties who knew she was dying had become depressed. Suddenly she raised her arms, her face lit up, and her eyes opened wide. She acted as though she were seeing someone she hadn't seen in a long time. She said, "Oh Katie, Katie." At this point, she roused from her comatose state. She seemed happy and died immediately after her vision.[6]

There were several Katies in this woman's family: a half-sister, an aunt, and a friend. All were dead.

What this case demonstrates is a rise in mood elevation after an encounter with a deceased loved one. This is a common occurrence, including feelings of serenity, joy, and peace.

Those who believe in life after death and the existence of another world are more apt to have comforting deathbed visions.

Some dying patients have visions of another world. A seventy-year-old woman said she saw the gates of heaven opening. They were shining tall portals. There were shining lights, much brighter than here. Everything looked so bright.[7]

Osis and Haraldsson, after examining thousands of deathbed visions and conducting numerous face-to-face interviews, conclude that the evidence strongly suggests life after death.

The Near-Death Experience

My interest in the near-death experience (NDE) goes back some two decades. Esther, a seventy-year-old Jewish lady, initially sparked it when she said to me in an agitated and angry voice, "Why didn't they let me stay? I was in such a beautiful place." Esther was angry with the medical team who had resuscitated her and brought her back to life. Esther had had a heavenly vision and she had not wanted to come back to a physical existence in a worn-out body. Harry, a man in his sixties, also stimulated my interest in the NDE. He shared with me that he had experienced a cardiac arrest while on the operating table and had left his body. As a result of this experience, he told me, "I will never again fear death. When I died, I felt a deep sense of peace, joy, and no pain." During Harry's brief NDE, he was healed of his fear of death and enjoyed feeling the peace that passes all understanding.

If Esther and Harry were transformed by their NDEs, how many others have been so influenced? In a Gallup poll taken in 1990, it was reported that 22 million U.S. adults have had a NDE. Since 1975, when Raymond Moody, Jr., M.D., published his book *Life After Life*,[8] the NDE has emerged as an object of study, research, and increasing public interest. In 1992, the Reader's Digest Association published a beautifully illustrated volume on "Life Beyond Death," and then in the March 31, 1997, issue, *U.S. News and World Report* featured a cover story article on the NDE. Dozens of books and numerous articles, by both near-death experiencers and scholarly writers, have been published.

Why should there be such an interest in the NDE? The NDE has addressed several issues that are of vital concern to most human beings: namely, the experience of dying and death, the afterlife, and what life might be like in that realm.

Though I have always maintained a Christian perspective on the afterlife, the NDE has filled in blind spots and greatly illuminated my own viewpoint. A NDE experience may contain the following:

1. A sense of being dead
2. Peace and painlessness
3. Out-of-body experience (OBE)
4. Tunnel experience

5. People of light
6. The being of light
7. Life review
8. Reluctance to return
9. Personality transformation

All nine stages are not experienced by all who have a NDE. The initial stages are the most common, although stage nine is experienced, in one degree or another, by all NDErs.

In order that the reader may get a feel for an NDE and its stages, I will quote at length from the case of Vicki. Kenneth Ring reported this case in his NDE research with the blind.[9] Ring relates that Vicki is a forty-three-year-old married woman who has been blind since birth. She tells of an event that occured when she wes twenty-two. She was in an emergency room of a hospital, having been seriously injured in an automobile accident. She found herself floating on the ceiling of the emergency room looking down on the medical team working on her body.

> "I knew it was me. I was pretty thin then. I was pretty thin and tall. I didn't know the body I saw was mine. Initially then I perceived I was up in the ceiling and thought, well that's kind of weird. What am I doing up here? And I thought, well that must be me. Am I dead? I just briefly saw this body and knew it must be mine because I wasn't in it."

So far, Vicki had had an out-of-body experience and a sense that she might be dead.

After this, Vicki recalls going up through the ceiling of the hospital until she was above the roof of the building. At this point, she had a brief panoramic view of her surroundings. She felt exhilarated and delighted in her freedom of movement. Then Vicki began to hear sublimely beautiful harmonica music akin to the sound of wind chimes.

The next thing Vicki discovered was that she had been sucked head-first into a tube and felt she was being pulled up into it. Though the enclosure was dark, Vicki was aware that she was moving toward light. As she reached the opening of the tube, the music she had heard earlier seemed to be transformed into hymns, and then she "rolled out" to find herself lying on grass. Trees, flowers, and a vast number of people surrounded her. She was in a place of tremendous light, and that light was something that could be felt as well as seen. The light conveyed love, and the people she saw were bright and reflected that love. "Everyone was made of light including myself. Love was everywhere, and it came from the grass, trees, and birds."

Vicki then became aware of five persons she had known in life who were welcoming her to this place. Debby and Diane were Vicki's blind classmates who had died at ages eleven and six. In life they had been profoundly retarded, but here they appeared bright, beautiful, and healthy. Vicki reports seeing two of her childhood caretakers, a couple named Mr. and Mrs. Zilk, both of whom had also previously died.

Finally, she saw her grandmother who had essentially raised her and had died two years earlier. The grandmother reached out to hug Vicki. In all these encounters, no actual words were exchanged, but only feelings of love and welcome.

In the midst of this rapture, Vicki was overcome with a sense of total knowledge. Vicki had a feeling that she knew everything about life, about the plants, and about God.

As these revelations were unfolding, Vicki noticed that next to her was a figure whose radiance was far greater than any person she had so far encountered. Immediately, she recognized this to be Jesus. He greeted her tenderly while she conveyed her excitement to him about her newfound knowledge and her joy about being with him. Telepathically he communicated to her, "Isn't it wonderful? Everyone is beautiful here, and it fits together. But you can't stay here now. It's not your time to be here yet, and you have to go back!"

Vicki reacted with extreme disappointment and protested vehemently, "No, I want to stay with you." Jesus reassured her that she would come back, but for now she had to "go back and teach more about loving and forgiving."

When Vicki learned she had to go back and have children, she then was willing, for she desperately wanted to have children.

Before Vicki could leave, Jesus said to her these exact words: "But first watch this!" In a panoramic view, Vicki then saw her whole life unfold, from birth to the present moment. The Being of Light then gently commented on the significance of her actions and their repercussions.

The last thing Vicki remembers is that once the life review was complete, she heard the words, "You have to go back now." She then experienced "a sickening thud" and found herself back in her body, feeling heavy and full of pain.

Since this NDE occurred, when she was twenty-two, Vicki has had the children she had so desperately wanted.

What does the NDE have to say about life after death? Universally, those who have had a NDE are convinced that some form of afterlife awaits us all on the other side of death.

Here is what one NDEr had to say: "I know there is life after death. Nobody can shake my belief. I have no doubt. It's peaceful and nothing to be feared. I don't know what's beyond what I experienced, but it's plenty for me. I know that death is not to be feared, only dying."[10]

Many who have been through a NDE could echo this type of testimony. The NDE is one more powerful witness pointing in the direction of a life beyond the grave.

The After-Death Communication

The after-death communication (ADC) occurs when a deceased person makes contact with a closely bonded relative or friend. Such communications have been with us since ancient times. Cicero, a prominent Roman writer and philosopher (106–43 B.C.E.), records an ADC from a traveling companion who had been murdered by thieves. The message was to warn Cicero that the thieves would be at a certain location waiting to plunder and kill him.[11]

Some of the most well-known of all ADCs are the post-resurrection appearances of Jesus to his disciples. In his resurrected body, Jesus was able to appear and disappear at will. He was able to pass through closed doors (Jn. 20:26), walk with two disciples on the road to Emmaus, and then mysteriously disappear during the breaking of bread (Lk. 24:30–31).

Even as Jesus' post-resurrection appearances were a source of comfort and strength to his disciples, so are the ADCs that occur today.

I remember the great comfort Oscar received when his recently deceased wife appeared to him in a vision. Oscar, a ninety-year-old man, was in deep grief and was seemingly inconsolable until Carrie came to him, saying she was safe, happy, and waiting for him on the other side. Immediately, Oscar brightened up and once again embraced life with his customary vigor and enthusiasm.

Three weeks after my mother died, she appeared to me in the context of a vision during my early morning sleep. Talking through an old-fashioned telephone, she conveyed to me that she was happy, peaceful, safe, and secure in her new dwelling place. Though I had no worry or concern about my mother in the afterlife, her ADC was nevertheless a great blessing to me and confirmed my belief that there is a life after death.

In October 1988, Bill and Judy Gugenheim began their investigation of after-death communications. The major question they asked in their research was, Have you been contacted by someone who has died? When the research was finished, 3,300 accounts of ADCs were collected, of which 2,000 involved interviews.[12]

The Gugenheims identified twelve types of ADCs. They are as follows:

1. Sensing a presence: sentient ADCs
2. Hearing a voice: auditory ADCs
3. Feeling a touch: tactile ADCs

4. Smelling a fragrance: olfactory ADCs
5. Partial appearance: visual ADCs
6. Full appearance: visual ADCs
7. A glimpse beyond: ADC visions
8. Encounters at alpha: twilight ADCs
9. More than a dream: sleep state ADCs
10. Homeward bound: out-of-body ADCs
11. Person-to-person: telephone ADCs
12. Material matters: ADCs of physical phenomena

In the course of their research, the Gugenheims accumulated many accounts of ADCs. I will share two of these accounts.

Neil is a retired mail carrier in Mississippi. His nineteen-year-old son died suddenly in his sleep from a heart arrhythmia.

> For about a year and a half, I couldn't turn Ken loose because I couldn't believe that he was gone. I figured if I could just hold on to him in some way I could bring him back.

> I always planted beautiful flowers at my son's grave and kept them watered. I was kneeling down when out of the clear blue, Ken's voice came to me. It was happy and real joyful. I heard him loud and clear (externally), like he was standing there, and I felt his presence. I raised up on my knees and looked around, but there was no one else in the cemetery.

> Ken said, "Dad, it's me. I wish you would turn me loose, so that I could enjoy where I am. You and Mom always brought me up to be with God. Now you're keeping me from him and enjoying Heaven. I cannot reach the fulfillment that God wants for me, because you are holding me back. I would appreciate it if you would just turn me loose and let me enjoy it here."

> I just busted out crying because I couldn't believe it. So I said. "Alright, Ken, this is it then. Son, I'm going to turn you loose and let you go." I'm not saying it was easy, but it was the right thing to do. Then I just sat there and cried and asked God's forgiveness, and when I did, the whole burden in my heart raised up off of me. All the pain left and I felt peace in my heart. This reaffirmed my whole faith, and since that day I have drawn a whole lot closer to God.[13]

Another striking and touching ADC is from a mother named Laura, who lost her six-week-old son, Anthony, from SIDS:

> It had been a traumatic year. My mother had died in March and I was having real difficulties with her loss. It was a very hard

winter. I was living in Montana then, and my husband and I were separated during the 6 weeks of Anthony's life. I didn't even know what Sudden Infant Death Syndrome was at that time. I felt like I was in a void. It was like a nightmare.

Part of my despair was that Anthony had not been baptized. Someone had planted a seed in my mind that all babies who aren't baptized would burn in hell forever. I was frantic because the guilt was more than I could bear.

When I came home from the cemetery after his funeral, I went into my bedroom and turned the lights off. I sat on the bed for quite a while and emptied my mind of all thought. I went to a very tranquil place. It was like I was on a raft in still water, and the water became like a mirror, and I started feeling peace. Then beautiful rays of light came down toward me, and a stairway became visible.

Suddenly Christ appeared in an awesome form and size! I had gone to church all my life and been close to God and close to Christ, and I knew this was Him. He was solid and real–He was magnificent! He had long hair and was clothed in a long white robe.

Christ started descending the stairs and came all the way to the bottom. He extended His arm and had Anthony cradled in it. Anthony was whole again! He was perfect. He was my baby!

The message I got was that "Anthony's all right. He is home and he is safe." Now I knew my baby was with Christ. Then they faded and disappeared.

This answered the one big question that had been tearing me apart. It relieved my agony of not having him baptized. Since then I've never worried about where Anthony is–I know he has a special place with Christ.[14]

ADCs that allow a living person to see, hear a voice, or sense a presence are persuasive reminders that there is an afterlife beyond death. An uncluttered and quiet mind such as you may have during meditation or twilight sleep seems to facilitate the occurrence of an ADC.

Immortality

Immortality is the belief that human beings have a part of their nature that is deathless. The deathless part is the soul, which at death is set free from the limitations of a human body.

The Greeks held the doctrine of the immortal soul, but Plato developed it. Plato described his ideas about immortality in the *Phaeda,* a discourse on the last days of Socrates. He saw human beings participating in two worlds, the physical and the spiritual. He believed the physical to be inferior. Plato argued that matter was chaotic and kept the spiritual component from reaching its full expression in this life. Plato tended to devalue the human body and physical existence. Plato's widespread influence caused many to come to see the body as the prison house of the soul.

While the early church and church fathers believed in the immortality of the soul, they did not devalue the human body or physical existence. Because God had created both worlds, they affirmed both worlds as good. This notion is eloquently stated in the Nicene Creed.

The Gnostic heresy was a movement in the early church that not only devalued the body but also taught that it was evil.

How does all this affect the doctrine of immortality? It has a profound influence in that it fails to see the physical life as a training ground for the spiritual life. Additionally, the body is honorable in that it is also a reflector of the divine image. The teaching of Christianity is the opposite of Hinduism and Buddhism, which hold that physical life is an illusion (Maya) and, therefore, escape to Nirvana is far better.

The physical and the spiritual realms are interconnected. They are both important dimensions in living a life of fullness.

Jesus and Paul taught the immortality of the soul. Jesus taught his disciples not to fear those who could kill the body but could not kill the soul (Mt. 10:28).

Paul, in the rich imagery of a tentmaker, declared, "For we know that if the earthly tent we live in is destroyed, we have a building from God, a house not made with hands, eternal in the heavens" (2 Cor. 5:1). Both of these passages teach the indestructibility of the soul, but Paul goes on to identify the soul as a creation of God.

What about the preexistence of the soul? Plato believed in the preexistence of the soul and that people's capacities were influenced by the soul they inhabited. He believed that at birth memories of the preexistent soul life were forgotten.

Jesus believed in the preexistence of his soul. In one discussion with the Pharisees he stated, "Before Abraham was, I am" (Jn. 8:58). If our souls existed before birth, then we can state with great certainty that, indeed, the soul is immortal.

Paul ties in the idea of immortality with a victory over death, "When...this mortal body puts on immortality, then the saying that is written will be fulfilled: 'Death has been swallowed up in victory'" (1 Cor. 15:54).

The Christian idea of immortality is both a positive and a life-affirming assertion. It calls us to be citizens of two worlds: the physical and the spiritual. The spiritual world will reach its greatest fulfillment as we move beyond the gates of death into the kingdom of heaven.

Resurrection

The resurrection of the dead is a highly prominent and fundamental doctrine of Christianity. New Testament writers unanimously assert that Christ's resurrection from the dead is what gives the Christian faith meaning, aliveness, and vitality. Paul declares that without resurrection, our faith is in vain (1 Cor. 15:14).

The resurrection of the dead is an important teaching of the Christian church. It boldly asserts that through faith one may participate in and look forward to a personal day of resurrection.

What is the foundation of such hope? The bodily resurrection of Jesus Christ from the dead and subsequent appearances to his disciples and other followers are key factors. Furthermore, the Christian church accepts the resurrection as an event that had taken place in a historical setting. The resurrection is not a mere philosophical speculation because of its historical character.

In his first letter to the Corinthians, Paul devotes the fifteenth chapter to an enlightening discussion of the resurrection. Paul notes the historical appearance of Christ as well as the mystery, nature, and characteristics of the resurrected body, including the dynamic and transforming changes the resurrection will have on all who experience it. In this discussion, Paul contrasts the earthly body and the heavenly body. He asserts that the changeover from the former to the latter will occur "in a moment, in the twinkling of an eye." All of this is very much in accord with people's accounts of near-death experiences, which report that at the moment of death, their earthly body is sloughed off and they find themselves in a profoundly different, nonphysical body.

Different aspects of resurrected life are illustrated when Jesus encounters the Sadducees and when Jesus reveals that God does not recognize a state of death.

The Sadducees presented the case of a woman who had successively been married to seven brothers, all of whom preceded her in death. Then the woman died. The Sadducees asked Jesus, "In the resurrection, then, whose wife of the seven will she be?" The Sadducees received an unexpected answer. Jesus told them that in the resurrection "they neither marry nor are given in marriage, but are like angels in heaven." Jesus went on to say that "[God] is God not of the dead, but of the living." After hearing these teachings, the Sadducees went away in silence (Mt. 22:23–33).

What can we learn from these teachings? Jesus tells us that heavenly life is profoundly different from earthly life. Instead of marriage, all become as angelic beings. Once again, there is a striking parallel with the NDE accounts and also with deathbed visions. In the latter, angels come (usually in the form of departed relatives) to escort their loved one to the heavenly realm. Angels are beings of light and messengers of God who are actively involved in deeds of kindness, compassion, and love.

The second teaching of Jesus reveals that God does not recognize a state of death. Abraham, Isaac, and Jacob are not dead; they are living in a different state than when on earth. Since God is the God of the living, it means that what we call death is only a transition to another life lived in the presence of God, Jesus, and a vast multitude of people who radiate love and light.

A second passage is a parable told by Jesus about a rich man who lived in sumptuous luxury and a poor man who begged for crumbs at the rich man's gate. This story also gives us valuable insights about the nature of resurrected life (Lk. 16:19–31). When the poor man (whose name was Lazarus) died, the angels carried him away into Abraham's bosom. In this place he found comfort and solace. Not so with the rich man, for when he died, he found himself in Hades, a place of fiery torment. In Hades the rich man was able to look up and see Abraham and Lazarus. The rich man appealed to Abraham to send Lazarus to him and dip the end of his finger in water to cool off his tongue, but Abraham responded and said, "Child, remember that during your lifetime you received your good things, and Lazarus in like manner evil things; but now he is comforted here, and you are in agony" (16:25). Abraham went on to explain to the rich man that there was a great chasm between the abode of comfort and the abode of Hades, which could not be crossed over.

This parable yields two important insights about afterlife. First, it tells us that there are different levels in the afterlife. The level where the self-centered rich man found himself is a place of regret, sorrow, and anguish. It is akin to the Hebrew concept of Sheol, or Hades; souls in this level exist in a gray and loveless type of atmosphere.

In sharp contrast is Abraham's bosom, a place of comfort, love, and peace. We have come to know this level as paradise or heaven. Here, the souls are animated, loving, caring, learning, and growing. They bask in the glory of God and are clothed in radiant white robes.

How many levels are there in the afterlife? There may be many levels, for Jesus taught, "In my Father's house there are many dwelling places" (Jn. 14:2).

If the afterlife is a place to grow in oneness and union with God, then the dwelling places might be stages along the way in our quest for full spiritual maturity.

A second teaching of the parable is that there are consequences to the way we live our lives. In his self-absorbed lifestyle, the rich man paid no attention to the poor beggar at his gate. The rich man had no time, no mercy, and no bread to offer the diseased and starving beggar. When the rich man died, he had no attitudinal change. He was still the self-centered man he had been on earth. In the afterlife, the rich man was dealing with the consequences of his self-centered lifestyle.

One of the aspects of afterlife is a life review. Biblical writers call attention to a judgment time when the deeds of a lifetime are reviewed, both good and evil. In NDE accounts, it is typically a panoramic motion-picture presentation of all the events from cradle to grave. In this review one feels the consequences of both good and evil attitudes as well as deeds.

The obvious implication of all this is that we who now live in the earthly sphere should seek to live a life filled with love for God, neighbor, and ourselves. In the NDE accounts, the life review is nonjudgmental, and guilt is absorbed by the richness of God's mercy and infinite forgiveness. The emphasis is on learning from past sins and mistakes and getting a fresh start in life.

Do the dead rise up? Is the earthly body transformed into a heavenly body?

"Listen, I will tell you a mystery...[W]e will all be changed, in a moment, in a twinkling of an eye, at the last trumpet. For the trumpet will sound, and the dead will be raised imperishable" (1 Cor. 15:51–52).

I thrill at these triumphant words! It is another compelling piece of evidence that the dead will be raised to an afterlife.

Poetry and Afterlife

What does poetry have to say about an afterlife? There is such abundance of poetry that speaks directly or indirectly about the existence of an afterlife that I have carefully pondered what to include and what to exclude. In the selection, I hope to help the reader view eternity through the visions of three gifted visionary poets.

What is a poet? A poet is one with a visionary imagination. He or she sees beyond this sensate and material world into the celestial and eternal world. In this process the poet uses metaphorical language and imaginative intuition. This poetry needs to be read, reread, and pondered so that one may come away with fresh meaning and illumination.

Poetry is provocative because it may evoke several meanings. One of the rewards of reading poetry is to see what meanings it will evoke in you.

The Divine Comedy

This classical poem is a superb work of art. It is also a poem of spontaneous passion, yet it is carefully organized and planned.

Dante Alighieri was born in Florence, Italy, in 1265, and died in 1321. He spent the first thirty-six years of his life in Florence and the last twenty in exile. He was bright, intellectual, creative, and he wrote both prose and poetry. He was actively involved in the current moral, religious, and political issues of his day.

In *The Divine Comedy,* Dante pictures afterlife as consisting of three locations: the inferno, the purgatorio, and the paradiso.

Dante's guide through the inferno and purgatorio is Virgil, a wise and respected poet who had lived centuries before in ancient Rome. The first part of their arduous journey takes them to the portals of hell where a sign states that all who enter here can bid farewell to hope.[15] It is a place of woe where souls suffer from a variety of unrepented mortal sins. As Virgil and Dante journey on, they hear loud cries and laments. Dante feels great anguish for the miserable souls encountered in the ten circles and layers of hell. Dante observes a glowing radiance above, which is Christ descending into limbo after his crucifixion.

As Virgil and Dante conclude their journey through the inferno, Virgil admonishes Dante, "Bear well in your mind what you have learned of cares to come, when you shall stand before the journey of the pattern of your life."[16]

The process of learning your life pattern in the loving presence of the one who sees all souls is very much like the life reviews reported by near-death experiencers. Dante's insights are very remarkable for one who lived in the late Middle Ages!

Can one pass from hell into purgatory? Presumably so, for why else would Christ visit hell if not to redeem souls that are repentant, trusting, and ready to receive God's mercy and grace? It seems entirely possible that Dante thought such a move from hell to purgatory could happen.

As Virgil and Dante leave the dismal pit of hell, they come to the kingdom of the purgatorio. Here, Dante breaks into a song that gives the purpose of the purgatorio:

"I will sing of the second kingdom, in which the human spirit cures itself and becomes fit to leap into Heaven."[17]

In order to ascend to the summit of Mount Purgatory, one must climb a stairway that goes through seven cornices, each representing a mortal sin. Souls at the seven cornices are being purged of the sins of pride, envy, anger, sloth, avarice, gluttony, and promiscuity.[18]

At the summit of Mount Purgatory one reaches the earthly paradise of Eden, which is the place to take the leap into heaven.

As Virgil and Dante ascend the stairway of Mount Purgatory, they encounter talkative souls who implore Dante to stop and talk with them. Dante finds that souls in the purgatorio are "lit up," though some more brightly than others. All, by the grace of God, are involved in a redemptive process that leads to the paradiso.

Before reaching the paradiso, Virgil departs, and Beatrice becomes Dante's guide. Because Beatrice dwells in paradise, she is a knowledgeable guide, well suited to escort Dante into the mystery and beauty of heaven.

Heaven is made up of angelic orders and virtues. The virtues encountered in heaven are faith; hope; love; prudence; courage; justice; moderation; a combination of faith, hope, and love; angels; and all virtues combined. Beatrice embodies all the ten virtues of heaven along with other saints such as the Blessed Virgin Mary and Saint Bernard.[19]

As Beatrice and Dante pass through the splendor of heaven with its radiant stars and shining virtues, Dante is enthralled and declares, "In that light a man becomes as such that it is impossible he should turn away even to look at any other thing."[20]

Everything is centered on God, whom all souls praise and glorify. Once again, souls motivated to seek a closer union with God ascend to stars and virtues of greater brilliance and intensity until they reach the tenth level, which combines all virtues. Here, one reaches the true paradise of the redeemed and unites with the Divine Essence.

Dante's *Divine Comedy* reflects the cultural, moral, political, and religious issues of the late Middle Ages. We should view it in this light while appreciating its superb insights and revelations.

William Blake's Poetry

William Blake, born in London, England, on November 28, 1757, was the second of five children born to James and Catherine Blake. At age four, Blake had a vision of God. He later saw a tree full of angels at Pecktham Rye. In 1787, Robert Blake, William's favorite brother, died. Blake saw Robert clapping his hands for joy as he ascended through the ceiling.[21]

Blake, in addition to being well educated, was a poet and was trained as a printer, painter, and engraver. He was gifted with rare intuition and a vivid imagination. To Blake, visionary imagination was the doorway to eternity. Blake believed that if man would make a friend or companion to the visionary image, he would arise from his grave and meet the Lord in the air.

Blake's dream was to restore each man to the ancient golden age where visionary imagination, love, and intuition would be the center of a life of joy and fullness. He had a profound intuitive grasp of human psychology, enabling him to have deep insights into the nature and behavior of humankind. Blake used his considerable talents and gifts to create imaginative poetry, prose, paintings, and engravings.

Blake's works of art can inspire and transport us into a spiritual world of angels, divine beings, and heaven. Through his work, we may leave the material world and dwell in eternity through the power of our visionary imagination.

I have selected a few examples of Blake's poetry that I believe picture the afterlife.

Land of Dreams
Awake, awake, my little boy!
Thou wast thy Mother's only joy,
Why dost thou weep in gentle sleep?
Awake! Thy Father dost thou keep.
O, what land is the land of dreams?
What are its mountains and what are its streams?
O, Father I saw my Mother there,
Among the lilies by water's fair.
Among the lambs clothed in white,
She walk'd with her Thomas in sweet delight.
I wept for joy like a dove I mourn,
O, when shall I again return?[22]

Eternity
He who binds to himself a joy
Does the winged life destroy
But he who kisses the joy as it flies
Lives in eternity's sunrise.[23]

To Morning
O, Holy Virgin! clad in purest white,
Unlock Heaven's Golden Gates, and issue forth,
Awake the dawn that sleeps in Heaven, let light
Rise from the chambers of the east, and bring
The honeyed dew that cometh on waking day.
O, radiant morning salute the sun,
Round like a huntsman to the chase, and, with
The buckskin'd feet appear upon the hills.[24]

Much of Blake's poetry is eschatological, dealing with the end of life and with death. There are an abundance of references to eternity and heaven. His paintings and etchings reveal various aspects of afterlife.

I especially like Blake's painting of the death of a good old man. It shows two angels escorting the man's soul to heaven. This particular vision is Christian in orientation. The presence of the Bible and the bread and wine symbolize the old man's faith.[25]

Other visionary paintings of Blake include the union of body and souls, the fate of lustful souls in Dante's *Inferno,* and a mystical vision of Blake in which a hand appears coming down from heaven.

Blake's visions of afterlife in poetry and paintings are extraordinary revelations, giving us a window into eternity. It is common, if not universal, that every person has a visualization of what will happen to him or her after death. This vision affects all that he does in life.

Emily Dickinson's Poetry

Emily Dickinson was born in Amherst, Massachusetts, on December 10, 1830, and died on May 15, 1886. She spent her entire life in her father's house and gradually withdrew into seclusion. Except for seven anonymous verses, her poems, which numbered 1,775, remained unpublished until after her death.

Dickinson's poetry, like herself, are both concealing and revealing. I have selected three of her poems that reflect her thoughts on the afterlife.

> 1. Heaven is so far of the mind
> that were the mind dissolved
> the site—of it—by architect
> could not again be proved.
> 'Tis vast as our capacity
> as fair—as our idea—
> to him of adequate desire
> no further 'tis than here.[26]

> 2. Heaven has different signs—to me—
> sometimes, I think that noon
> is but a symbol of the place
> and when again, at dawn.

> A mighty look runs
> round the world.
> And settles in the hills—
> an awe if it should be like that
> upon the ignorant steals.

> The orchard when the sun is on—
> the triumph of the birds
> when they together victory make—
> some carnivals of clouds.

> The rapture of a finished day—
> returning to the west
> all these remind us of the place
> that men call "Paradise"—
> Itself be fairer—we suppose—
> but how ourself, shall be

adorned, for a superior grace—
not yet, our eyes can see.[27]

3. Behind me—dips eternity—
before me—immortality—
myself—the term between
death, but the drift of
eastern grey
dissolving into dawn away,
before the west began—

'Tis kingdoms—afterward—they say
in perfect—pauseless monarchy—
whose prince—is son of none
himself—his dateless dynasty—
himself—himself diversity—
in duplicate divine—

'Tis miracle before me—then
'tis miracle—behind—between—
a crescent in sea—
with midnight to the north of her—
and midnight to the south of her—
and maelstrom—in the sky.[28]

In the first poem Dickinson perceived that heaven is a state of mind. In the second poem she sees the signs of heaven in nature. In the third poem she sees herself surrounded by eternity in an everlasting kingdom—dynasty—that has been made perfect by its monarch. Such a kingdom, she declares, is a miracle.

Emily Dickinson's visionary and insightful poetry gives us a beautiful and picturesque view of eternity.

Mysticism and Afterlife

What is the relationship between mysticism and the afterlife? In the ecstatic moments of the mystical life, the mystic has glimpsed a world beyond the senses. In this new dimension that is beyond space and time, he or she may experience the wonder, joy, and bliss of heaven. The blissful experience of the mystic is very similar to those of near-death experiencers, whose experiences I have already discussed earlier in this chapter.

Who is a mystic? A mystic is one who has attained or seeks to attain union with God. Jesus had attained this experience and called it oneness with the Father (Jn. 10:38, 17:21). Jesus intended that all of his followers attain the mystical experience of "oneness with the Father." As we will see in the mystics to be considered in this section, the mystical experience goes beyond the physical, emotional, and mental realm in which we are so accustomed to dwelling. Because of the mystic's urgent longings and yearnings for God, the mystic is willing to undergo a period of preparatory spiritual exercises to reach the paradise that lies hidden within the soul. Most mystics practice some form of contemplation or meditation.

A mystic lives between three worlds: the world of time and eternity, the world of becoming and being, and the world of multiplicity and unity.[29] As an aspiring mystic, I recognize the challenge of living in the in-between area of these three worlds. I am driven by deep inner longings to follow the path of mystics.

There are three stages generally recognized by those who follow the mystical path. The first stage is purgation. This involves a cleansing and refining process aimed at removing all blocks standing in the way of an intimate relationship with God. For most mystics this is an ongoing, life-long process. In general, the work of purgation moves a person from self-centeredness to God-centeredness.

The second stage, illumination, is marked by the flooding of the personality with divine light. Walt Whitman described the light as "rare and untellable." Hildegard said the light that appeared to her was more brilliant than the brightness around the sun. St. Theresa of Avila thought the light to be infused brightness, a light that knows no night, and nothing ever disturbs it.[30]

Illuminating experiences are not as rare as one might think. Illumination can happen dramatically and unexpectedly. Jesus promised illumination to humankind when he said, "Blessed are the pure in heart, for they will see God" (Mt. 5:8).

The third stage and final goal of mystical experience is union with God. St. John of the Cross describes this as a union of the soul with the trinity of love, power, and wisdom, of which love is the first cause and love is the principal.[31] In uniting with the Godhead, we are restored to the fullness of all that it means to be created in God's image. This means sharing God's love, power, and wisdom as well as God's compassion, mercy, joy, and peace.

In union with God, we do not lose our individuality; rather, our individuality is transformed by the abiding presence of God within the soul. Union with God need not wait until the day of final rapture, but according to the mystics, it can happen in the here and now.

In order to better understand mysticism, we will consider the lives of three mystics. Emphasis will be placed on the mystics' conceptions of afterlife.

Meister Eckhart

Meister Eckhart was born about 1260 in the province of Thurngia, Germany. He was one of several Rhineland mystics. Because he did not hesitate to criticize self-centeredness and the lack of compassion for the poor, he soon got in trouble with church authorities, resulting in the church's condemning him in 1327.

The profound insights of Meister Eckhart about the nature of God, human beings, and eternity were likely gained during times of mystical revelations.

He was a popular preacher. His sermon "Holiness of Being" contains pertinent insights about afterlife and the destiny of martyrs who perished by the sword.

Here is the gist of the sermon.

God never destroys without giving something better in its place. The martyrs are dead and have lost life, but they have received Being. To the extent that anything has Being, it resembles God. Being is eternal. God is aware of nothing but Being, and Being is a circle for Him. To the extent that our life is Being, it is in God.

Our life may be very small, but if we grasp it as Being, then it is nobler than anything ever attained.

People should go willingly toward their death, so that a better form of being is theirs.

Dead things become alive through the power of God's Being. To God nothing dies, for all things live in Him.

Time is mortal. Heaven is eternal and it knows nothing about time.[32]

Eckhart finds the nature of afterlife to be a state of being; death is not to be feared. In fact, we should go to it willingly, for it will give us a better form of being.

Being is granted us through the power of God. It is invisible and formless. To the extent that we have being, we are timeless, eternal, heavenly, and resemble God.

Today's society places emphasis on doing. The meaning of a human being is defined by his or her "doings." Human accomplishments are commendable. However, they are more powerful and enduring and satisfying when they flow out of a sense of being. Take a moment and scan yourself. Are you rooted in being or doing? Being is an internal state. It is the state that gives us peace and serenity during this life and at the end of our days. Being is the state of afterlife.

Why is this so? It is because God is pure being and has called each human being to rest in this state.

The Cloud of Unknowing

The author of this work is unknown, but it is believed that he was a monk living in England in the middle of the fourteenth century when the Roman Catholic Church was ready to persecute and condemn anyone suspected of heresy. The work was addressed to the common man so that he might realize the core of his inner nature and God's.

The author first deals with the many obstacles a man must overcome, such as misleading thoughts, wanderings of a curious mind, unconscious associations and strong promptings of the imagination, bonds of senses, and memories that bind to the past. The author states that God may not be reached through thought, but through love. "Lift up your heart to God with a meek stirring of love, seeking God himself, and none of his created things."[33]

A major theme occurring over and over again in the author's work is the "cloud of unknowing." No matter what you do, this cloud is between you and your God, and you will not see or feel God.[34] If you are ever to see or feel God, states the author, it will be in the cloud of unknowing.

To pierce the thick cloud of unknowing, use a sharp dart of longing love. The sharp dart may reach the heart of God, who is full of love, graciousness, and mercy. God wants nothing more than for you to listen to God, and then God will chatter on more and more.

The author recommends the selection of a short word, such as God or love. This word may be used as a shield or spear; use this word to strike down thoughts of every kind as well as to beat on the cloud above.[35]

The author sees that the higher part of the contemplative life that takes place in the cloud of unknowing is a way of blindly beholding the naked being of God.[36] Contemplation will continue beyond this life and into eternity.

Athough man may never have clear sight in this life, it need not stop him from meeting and experiencing God in the cloud of unknowing.

The author has provided the discerning reader with a useful guidebook on how to approach and experience God. The approach to God is through love and not thoughts. The approach needs to move beyond mental and sensory obstacles. In the quest for God, these must be laid aside. The approach to God takes place in the darkness of a cloud of unknowing. In this sense the seeker may one day behold a veiled God.

The use of a short word can help one to keep attention focused on God, as well as to strike down intruding thoughts. The author's approach to seeking God seems in accord with the way many of us might encounter God. I agree with the author that love is the supreme means by which God comes to us and we to God.

St. John of the Cross

St. John was born on June 24, 1542, near Avila, Spain, and died December 14, 1591. In 1563 he joined the Carmelite Order, and in 1579 he began to write *The Ascent to Mt. Carmel.* This work became a spiritual classic and guidebook for those who seek union with God. Thomas Merton believed St. John to be the greatest of all mystical theologians.

Living during the dark days of the Spanish Inquisition, St. John consequently couched much of his writings in metaphorical language. His poem *Dark Night of the Soul* is unexcelled in expressing the beauty, mystery, and wonder that goes into the union of the lover with his beloved.

> On a dark night, Kindled in love with yearnings–oh, happy chance!–
> I went forth without being observed, My house being now at rest...
>
> In the happy night, In secret, when none saw me,
> Nor I beheld aught, Without light or guide, save that which burned in my heart.
>
> This light guided me More surely than the light of noonday
> To the place where he (well I knew who!) was awaiting me–A place where none appeared.
>
> Oh, night that guided me, Oh, night more lovely than the dawn,
> Oh, night that joined Beloved with lover, Lover transformed in the Beloved!
>
> Upon my flowery breast, Kept wholly for himself alone,
> There he stayed sleeping, and I caressed him, And the fanning of the cedars made a breeze...
>
> I remained, lost in oblivion; My face I reclined on the Beloved.
> All ceased and I abandoned myself, Leaving my cares forgotten among the lilies.[37]

In these beautiful lines of poetry, St. John describes the process of union with God. Notice the complete detachment from the sensate world.

Metaphors such as the dark night, going out unseen, and the house being stilled indicate detachment from mental, emotional, and physical stimuli.

A second observation is guidance by an inner light. Every soul has a divine inner light. Once this light is turned on and allowed to burn brightly, it will naturally draw one to its source, which is the divine lover.

Deep within our hearts, after the fog has lifted, every soul seeks to be united with this lover, "the Beloved."

Once there has been a union between the lover and his beloved, there is nothing to do but to rest and be in a state of pure bliss and enjoyment of each other's presence. So intimate is this relationship that John speaks of caressing his lover and losing track of himself and all his cares.

The only outcome of such a rapturous union with the divine lover is transformation. All souls who meet with God in an intimate union are all forever changed.

The first time I read St. John's *Dark Night of the Soul,* I committed it to memory. Over the years I have found it to be a source of beauty and inspiration, ever urging me on toward a fuller and more intimate relationship with my divine lover.

Separation of Body and Spirit (the Beginning Stage of Afterlife)

What happens at the time of death to the indwelling immortal spirit? Are there those among us who have observed this mysterious event? Those blessed with the gift of clairvoyance have sometimes been eyewitnesses to the separation of body and spirit.

I found two fascinating accounts while reading through Ken Ring's book *Life at Death.* He had selected these two accounts from Robert Crookall's books.[38]

Estelle Roberts described her husband's transition. "I saw his spirit leave the body. It emerged from his head and gradually molded itself into an exact replica of his earth-body. It remained suspended about a foot above his body, lying in the same position, i.e., horizontal, and attached to it by a cord to the head. Then the cord broke and the spirit-form floated away passing through the wall."[39]

The next account is provided by a twentieth-century physician, R.B. Hout, who witnessed the death of his aunt.

> My attention was called to something immediately above the physical body, suspended in the atmosphere about 2 feet above the bed. At first, I could distinguish nothing more than a vague outline of hazy, fog-like substance. There seemed to be only a

mist held there suspended, motionless, but as I looked, very gradually there grew into my sight a denser, more solid, condensation of this inexplicable vapor. Then I was astonished to see definite outlines presenting themselves, and soon I saw this fog-like substance was assuming a human form.

Soon I knew that the body I was seeing resembled that of the physical body of my aunt. The astral body hung suspended horizontally a few feet above the physical counterpart. I continued to watch. And the spirit-body now seemed complete to my sight. I saw the features plainly, they were very similar to the physical face, except that a glow of peace and vigor were expressed instead of age and pain. The eyes were closed, as though in tranquil sleep, and a luminosity seemed to radiate from the spirit body.

As I watched the suspended spirit body, my attention was called, again intuitively, to a silver like substance that was streaming from the head of the physical body to the head of the spirit "Double." Then I saw the connection between the two bodies. As I watched, the thought, "the silver cord" kept running through my mind. I knew, for the first time, the meaning of it. This "silver cord" was the connecting link between the physical and spiritual bodies, even as the umbilical cord unites the child to its mother.

The cord was round, being an inch in diameter. The color was a translucent luminous silver radiance. The cord seemed alive with vibrant energy. I could see the pulsations of light stream along the course of it, from the direction of the physical body to the spirit "Double." With each pulsation the spirit body became more alive and denser, whereas the physical body became quieter and more nearly lifeless. By this time the features were very distinct. The life was all in the astral body, the pulsations of the cord had stopped. I looked at the various strands of the cord as they spread out, fanlike at the base of the skull. Each strand snapped. The final severance was at hand. A twin process of death and birth was about to ensue. The last connecting strand of the silver cord snapped and the spirit body was free.

The spirit body, which had been horizontal before, now rose. The closed eyes opened and a smile broke from the radiant features. She gave a smile of farewell, then vanished from my sight. (The above phenomenon was witnessed by me as an entirely objective reality. The spirit forms I saw with the aid of my physical eyes.)[40]

The split-off of a spirit "double" resembling the features of the physical body is both fascinating and revealing. This gives an understanding of how we know and recognize loved ones and friends in afterlife. Another aspect is that the spirit body is luminous, radiant, free from age or pain, and may have a range of emotions, such as love, joy, and peace.

Dr. Hout's account makes mention of the silver cord connecting the physical and spiritual bodies. The knowledge of a silver cord goes back to the ancient sages of Israel who lived several centuries before the birth of Christ. The writer of Ecclesiastes counsels his readers to remember the creator "before the silver cord is snapped" (Eccl. 12:6a). When the silver cord has broken, it is a signal that death has occurred and the spirit body is free to make its ascent.

Near-death experiencers go through a similar process, but it is seldom reported, as they (the NDErs) are so involved in the many changes happening to them.

I see the beginning stage of afterlife, which is the out-of-body experience (OBE), as one more piece of evidence pointing to the existence of an afterlife.

In this chapter, we have taken a look at eight different pieces of evidence that point to the existence of an afterlife. This is by no means an inclusive list, but it presents some of the major players in the case for an afterlife.

If you have paid but scant attention to the possibility of an afterlife, this chapter has given you an opportunity to consider the various evidences that make a case for an afterlife.

For those who have believed in an afterlife prior to reading this chapter, it may serve to strengthen and fortify your belief. For those who have been nonbelievers or skeptics, it may open the door for a fresh look and perhaps a faith to believe in the reality of an afterlife.

It is faith that builds the bridge to envision an afterlife. As an inspired hymn writer put it, "There's a land that is fairer than day, and by faith we can see it afar."[41]

The subject of afterlife is rarely, if ever, discussed in today's society. Why is the topic of afterlife avoided? Are we uncomfortable, or do we lack knowledge? Perhaps it is a bit of both. An aim of this chapter is to open a door for discussion of the subject. It is my hope that I have dispelled the discomfort and anxiety that so often seem to attend the subject.

In my own case, I see entrance into afterlife as the beginning of the greatest adventure of a lifetime. Afterlife is just around the corner for each of us. Now is a good time to acquaint ourselves and firm up our beliefs about the mysteries of afterlife.

Epilogue

So let the way wind up the hill or down,
O'er rough or smooth, the journey will be joy:
Still seeking what I sought when but a boy,
New friendships, high adventure, and a crown.
I shall grow old but never lose life's zest
for the road's last turn will be the best.[1]

I can't imagine my life without a study library, yellow legal pad, bold black pen, and stimulating interpersonal relationships, all of which have become very important to me because they foster creativity and quality of life.

My study is a hallowed place. It is a place to withdraw, meditate, contemplate, dream, plan, compose, write, and generate ideas. It is a place to give birth to fresh images and see if they will fly.

The books that line my library shelves are friends, and I turn to them for inspiration, to broaden my horizons, to introduce me to new fields of inquiry, and to fortify me with pertinent information.

Sometimes I read a book for pure enjoyment–to escape into another world. Whatever, my books are a rich source of creative ideas and dreams.

Stimulating conversations with my wife, or with friends, are lifelines providing encouragement, meaning, and sometimes "a-ha" revelations.

To me, creative ventures such as writing and composing poetry keep life exciting and worthwhile.

In spite of physical limitations, does my present life have quality? To be sure. I am content to be where I am, and who I am, at this stage of my life!

My quality comes first from Being, and then from doing the things that bring meaning. I am blessed as I reach out to others, even as they reach out to me.

It is most important to me, as I journey through life, to make a contribution for the enrichment of my community and world.

I believe that my life has a divine plan and purpose. In some way each day I hope to be about the fulfillment of this plan and purpose. How well am I doing?

When I cross over to the other side and have my "life review," I'll let you know!

Notes

Introduction

[1]Albert Einstein, "What I Believe," *Forum* (October 1930).

Chapter 1: Discovering Spirituality

[1]Sydney M. Jourard, *The Transparent Self* (New York: D. Van Nostrand, 1964), 82–84.

[2]Victor E. Frankl, *The Doctor and the Soul* (New York: Alfred A. Knopf, 1968), 93–104. See also Victor Frankl's *Search for Meaning* (Boston: Beacon Press, 2000) for full details of how he survived the deprivations and horrors of a Nazi concentration camp.

[3]Herbert Benson, *Beyond the Relaxation Response* (New York: Time Book, 1984), 6–7. Herbert Benson, M.D., is one of the pioneers in mind-body studies. See also his book on the *Mind/Body Effect* (New York: Simon & Schuster, 1979).

[4]Rex Warner, trans., *The Confessions of St. Augustine* (New York: Penguin Books, 1963), 14. This autobiography records Augustine's passionate conversations with and intimate confessions to God.

[5]John Bunyan, *The Pilgrim's Progress*, rephrasing by Gladys N. Larson (Chicago: Covenant Press, 1984).

[6]Robert A Johnson, *He! A Contribution to Understanding Masculine Psychology* (New York: Harper & Row, 1974. The book is an in-depth study of the myth of the Holy Grail from a Jungian perspective.

[7]Mary Catherine Fish, "Letting Go," *Readers Digest* (May 1999): 198.

[8]Ibid., 222, 224.

Chaper 2: Models of Spirituality

[1]Nina Morgan, *Mother Teresa: Saint of the Poor* (Austin, Tex.: Steck Vaughn, 1998). The story of Mother Teresa's life, pertinent information, and quotes that I use are from this excellent pictorial book. All are easily located in this slender volume of forty-eight pages.

[2]Nevin Chawla, *Mother Teresa: The Authorized Biography* (Rockport, Mass.:, Element Books, 1992), xii–xiii. This comprehensive volume of Mother Teresa's life was written by a Hindu who was profoundly influenced by the unselfish life of Mother Teresa. Though Mother Teresa did not want a book written about her life, she nevertheless gave the author permission to contact key people who knew her life story.

[3]Ira Pope, *The Life and Work of Martin Luther King, Jr.* (New York: Scholastic, 1968). I have relied on this book for background information on the life of Martin Luther King, Jr.

[4]Ibid., 34–35.

[5]Coretta Scott King, *My Life with Martin Luther King, Jr.* (New York: Henry Holt, 1969; rev. ed., 1993), 1–13.

[6]Text of speech available online at http://www.stanford.edu/group/King/about_king/

[7]See Exodus 3–4 for a background of this period of Moses' life.

[8]See Exodus 16–34 for background on Moses' life in the wilderness and his growing intimacy with God.

[9]Martin Buber, *Between Man and Man* (Boston: Beacon Press, 1953), 1–17, 97. Buber's little book *I and Thou* was originally published (in German) in 1923.

[10]William C Ketchum, Jr., *Grandma Moses: An American Original* (New York: Smithmark Publishers, 1996). I have relied on chapter 1, "The Artist's Life," for background on Grandma Moses' life. This book also contains many of Grandma Moses' paintings in color.

[11]Ibid., 21.

[12]Mitch Albom, *Tuesdays with Morrie* (New York: Doubleday, 1997). Background information on the life and experiences of Morrie Schwartz are drawn from this book.

[13]Initially, I ignored and denied the diagnosis of diabetes. It was only when I accepted it that I learned to live with it.

[14]Albom, 164.

[15]Ibid., 166.

[16]Luke 15:11–24. This New Testament passage contains the parable of the prodigal son.

Chapter 3: Spirituality and Adversity

[1]John C. Katonah, *Rites of Passage: A Paradigm for Hospital Ministry* (Schaumberg, Ill.: Care Cassettes, College of Chaplains, September 1989). The College of Chaplains is now known as the Association of Professional Chaplains.

[2]Alan D. Randolph died Nov. 1, 1999, and I was a co-officiant at his funeral service. The writing that appears here was prior to his death.

[3]I obtained information about Alzheimer's from The Alzheimer's Association, 919 Michigan Ave., Suite 1000, Chicago, IL 60611.

[4]The interview with Fred (a fictitious name) took place on August 30, 1999. First names used in this book are not actual names unless they are members of my own family.

[5]Neal Olshan, *Power Over Your Pain Without Drugs* (New York: Rawson, Wade, 1980). This is a useful and practical sourcebook for anyone suffering chronic pain.

[6]Ibid., 161–94.

[7]Ibid., 112–13.

[8]Reynolds Price, *A Whole New Life* (New York: Maxwell MacMillan, 1994). This is a remarkable firsthand account of Price's journey with pain and his healing.

[9]Ibid., 42–43.

[10]Ibid., 76.

[11]Ibid., 159.

[12]Ibid., 192.

[13]John L. Maes, *Suffering, a Caregivers Guide* (Nashville: Abingdon Press, 1990), 29–31.

[14]Ibid., 89.

[15]Donald Oken, *Stress: Our Friend or Foe? Blueprint for Health* (Chicago: Blue Cross Association, 1974), vol. 25, no. 1.

[16]Gina Pera, "Stress and Health," *The Christian Home* (Dec.–Feb. 1981–82): 31.

Chapter 4: Spirituality, Imagination, and Healing

[1]Ranier Maria Rilke, *Letters to a Young Poet* (Novato, Calif.: New World Library, 2000), Letter #13.

[2]Barbara Hannah, *Active Imagination* (Boston: Siego Press, 1981), 9–11.

[3]Ibid., 149–53.

[4]Jeanne Achterberg, *Imagery in Healing* (Boston: Shambhala, 1985), 5. In my commentary on imagination in healing, Jeanne Achterberg's book has been a basic resource for me.

[5]Ibid., 49.

[6]Jean Houston, *The Search for the Beloved* (Los Angeles: Jeremy P. Tarcher, 1987), 4.

[7]Ibid., 7.

[8]Achterberg, 72.

[9]Jan Goodwin, "Amazing Grace," *Family Circle* (14 November 2000): 48.

[10]Norman Cousins, *The Healing Heart* (New York: Norton, 1983), 16.

[11]Achterberg, 172–73.

[12]Ibid., 169.

[13]Ibid., 170.

[14]Ibid., 170–71.

[15]Dean Ornish, *Love and Survival: The Scientific Basis for the Healing Power of Intimacy* (New York: Harper Collins, 1998), 23–71.

[16]Joyce Goodrich, "Healing and Meditation, Healing as a Unitive Experience," *CTRP (Consciousness Training and Research Project) Newsletter*, 17, no. 1 (May 1993): 3–4.

¹⁷Ibid., 7.

¹⁸Lawrence Le Shan, *The Medium, the Mystic and the Physicist* (New York: Viking Press, 1974). This book contains Le Shan's investigation of the paranormal. Out of this investigation he identified five types of healing.

¹⁹Ibid., 44.

²⁰Herbert Benson, *Relaxation Response* (Boston: G.K. Hall, 1976); see also his *Beyond the Relaxation Response* (New York: Time Books, 1984).

²¹Lawrence Le Shan, *How to Meditate* (Boston, Mass.: Little Brown, 1974), 58–60.

²²R. M. French, *The Way of a Pilgrim* (New York: Seabury Press, 1965). This book is the personal diary of a Russian pilgrim. It records his travels in nineteenth-century Russia and his quest to learn to pray without ceasing. It has become a classic of the spiritual life. To all who seek after a deeper Christian spirituality, this book is both fascinating and worthwhile. R. M. French translated the book from Russian into English.

²³Mike and Nancy Samuels, *Seeing with the Mind's Eye* (New York: Random House, 1975), 232. This wonderfully illustrated book is about the history, techniques, and uses of visualization.

²⁴Diane Goldner, *Infinite Grace: Where the Worlds of Science and Spiritual Healing Meet* (Charlottesville, Va.: Hampton Roads, 1999), 14.

²⁵Mark Beck, *The Theory and Practice of Therapeutic Massage* (New York: Milady, 1988), 12.

Chapter 5: Spirituality, Loss, and the Grief Process

¹J. William Worden, *Grief Counseling and Grief Therapy* (New York: Springer, 1982).

²I am indebted to the Carondelet Hospice Service, Tucson, Arizona, for their useful outline, summarizing feelings and physical sensations common in the bereaved.

Chapter 6: Spirituality and Preparation for the Final Journey

¹This epitaph can be found inscribed on many nineteenth-century gravestones. I first saw it on a gravestone in the abandoned ghost town of Caribou, Colorado, in 1966. I do not know the name of the author of this poem.

²Elisabeth Kübler-Ross, M.D., *On Life After Death* (Berkeley, Calif.: Celestial Arts, 1991), 23–37.

³Anya Foos-Graber, *Deathing* (York Beach, Me.: Nicolas-Hays, 1989).

⁴Don Campbell, *The Mozart Effect* (New York: Avon Books, 1997), 211, 217.

⁵Ibid., 216–17.

⁶Ibid., 209.

⁷Ibid., 95–97.

⁸The woman who witnessed her mother's homegoing escorted by two angels possessed clairvoyant powers, thus giving her spiritual eyesight.

Chapter 7: Spirituality, Transformation, and Afterlife

¹Karlis Osis and Erlendur Haraldsson, *At the Hour of Death* (New York: Avon Books, 1977), 2–3.

²Ibid., 15–16.

³Ibid., 3.

⁴Ibid., 40.

⁵Ibid., 43.

⁶Ibid., 61.

⁷Ibid., 166.

⁸Raymond Moody, *Life After Life* (New York: Bantam Books, 1976).

⁹Kenneth Ring and Sharon Cooper, "Near-death and Out of Body Experiences in the Blind. A Study of Apparent Eyeless Vision," *Journal of Near-Death Studies* (Winter 1997): 108–12.

¹⁰Kenneth Ring, *Lessons from the Light* (New York: Insight Books, 1998), 275.

¹¹Bill and Judy Guggenheim, *Hello from Heaven* (New York: Bantam Books, 1996), 9–10.

¹²Ibid., 16–19.

¹³Ibid., 308.

[14]Ibid., 302.

[15]Dante Alighieri, *Inferno,* ed. Thomas G. Bergen (New York: Appleton Century Crofts, 1948), 8.

[16]Ibid., 110.

[17]Dante Alighieri, *The Divine Comedy,* trans. C. H. Sisson, with notes and introduction by David H. Higgins (New York: Oxford University Press, 1980), 199.

[18]Ibid., 198.

[19]Ibid., 32–33.

[20]Ibid., 499.

[21]William Blake, in *Blake's Poetry and Designs,* selected and edited by Mary Lynn Johnson and John E. Grant (New York: W. W. Norton, 1979), xxviii, xxix.

[22]Ibid., 205.

[23]Ibid., 183.

[24]Ibid., 4.

[25]Mike and Nancy Samuels, *Seeing with the Mind's Eye* (New York: Random House, 1977), 205.

[26]Thomas H. Johnson, Selection and Introduction, *Final Harvest, Emily Dickinson's Poems* (Boston, Mass.: Little Brown, 1961), 82.

[27]Ibid., 145–46.

[28]Ibid., 181–82.

[29]Evelyn Underhill, *Practical Mysticism* (New York: E.P. Dutton, 1915), 40.

[30]Judith Cressy, *The Near-Death Experience: Mysticism or Madness?* (Hanover, Mass.: Christopher Publishing House, 1994), 73.

[31]Ibid., 73.

[32]Meister Eckhart, *Breakthrough! Meister Eckhart's Creation Spirituality, in New Translation* (Garden City, N.Y.: Image Books, 1980), 84–85.

[33]Ira Progoff, trans., *The Cloud of Unknowing,* with an introduction by Ira Progoff (New York: Dell, 1957).

[34]Ibid., 35–36.

[35]Ibid., 149.

[36]Ibid.

[37]See http://www.ccel.org/j/john_cross/dark_night.html for this translation by E. Allison Peers.

[38]Kenneth Ring, *Life at Death: A Scientific Investigation of the Near-Death Experience* (New York: Coward, McCann and Geoghegan, 1980), 226–27. The name of Crookall's book, for those interested in pursuing it, is *Out-of-the-Body Experiences* (London: Citadel Press, 1992).

[39]Ibid., 226.

[40]Ibid., 227.

[41]Sanford Bennett, "In the Sweet By and By," 1868.

Epilogue

[1]Henry Van Dyke's poem is quoted in slightly different forms and under different titles online and in anthologies. The poem's last lines in many sources is "My heart will keep the courage of the quest / And hope the road's last turn will be the best." One Web source for the work is http://www.theotherpages.org/poems/vandyke1.html.

Bibliography

This bibliography is not intended to be exhaustive. Rather, it represents only a few of the many volumes available in today's public libraries and bookstores. For the convenience of the reader, the books are categorized into various subjects.

Spirituality, Mysticism, and Soul

Alighieri, Dante. *Inferno.* Edited by Thomas G. Bergen. New York: Appleton Century Crofts, 1948.

Benson, Herbert. *Timeless Healing: The Power and Biology of Belief.* New York: Scribners, 1996.

Boehme, Jacob. *The Way to Christ.* Translated with an introduction by Peter Erb. New York: Paulist Press, 1978.

Brunton, Paul. *Discover Yourself.* York Beach, Me.: Samuel Weisser, 1971.

———. *The Secret Path: A Technique of Spiritual Self-Discovery for the Modern World.* New York: E. P. Dutton, 1935.

Buber, Martin. *Between Man and Man.* Boston: Beacon Press, 1953.

Bunyan, John. *The Pilgrim's Progress.* As retold by Gladys N. Larson. Chicago: Covenant Press, 1984.

Chawla, Nevin. *Mother Teresa: The Authorized Biography.* Rockport, Mass.: Element Books, 1998.

De Gaussade, Jean Purre. *Abandonment to Divine Provenience.* Translated by John Bevers. Garden City, N.Y.: Image Books, 1975.

Eckhart, Meister. *Breakthrough: Master Eckhart's Creation Spirituality, in New Translation.* Garden City, N.Y.: Image Books, 1980.

Fox, Matthew. *Original Blessing: A Primer in Creation Spirituality.* Santa Fe, N.M.: Bear and Co., 1983.

French, R. M., trans. *The Way of the Pilgrim.* New York: Seabury Press, 1965.

Green, Thomas H. *When the Well Runs Dry.* Notre Dame, Ind.: Ave Maria Press, 1979.

Gregory I, Pope. *Life and Miracles of St. Benedict.* Translated by Odo J. Zimmerman and Benedict R. Avery. Collegeville, Minn.: Liturgical Press, 1949.

Hall, Manly P. *The Mystical Christ: Religion as a Personal Spiritual Experience.* Los Angeles: Philosophical Research Society, 1951.

Herman, Nicolas (Brother Lawrence). *The Practice of the Presence of God.* Westwood, N.J.: Fleming H. Revell, 1958.

———. *The Practice of the Presence of God.* New Kensington, Pa.: Whitaker House, 1982.

Jaidar, George. *The Soul: An Owners Manual, Discovering the Life of Fullness.* New York: Paragon House, 1995.

James, William. *The Varieties of Religious Experiences.* New York: New American Library, 1958.

Johnson, Mary Lynn, and John E. Grant, eds. *Blake's Poetry and Designs.* New York: W. W. Norton, 1979.

Johnson, Robert A. *He! A Contribution to Understanding Masculine Psychology.* New York: Harper & Row, 1974.

Jorgen, Johannel. *St. Francis of Assisi Biography.* Translated by T. Oconne Slcane. Garden City, N.Y.: Image Books, 1935.

Julian of Norwich. *Revelations of Divine Love.* Translated with an introduction by M. L. del Mastro. Garden City, N.Y.: Image Books, 1977.

Katonah, John C. *Rites of Passage: A Paradigm for Hospital Ministry.* Schaumberg, Ill.: Care Cassettes, College of Chaplains, September 1989.

Kelsey, Morton T. *The Christian and the Supernatural.* Minneapolis: Augsburg, 1976.

Ketchum, William C., Jr. *Grandma Moses: An American Original.* New York: Smithmark, 1996.

King, Coretta Scott. *My Life with Martin Luther King, Jr.* New York: Henry Holt, 1969. Revised edition, 1993.

Le Shan, Lawrence. *The Medium, the Mystic, and the Physicist.* New York: Viking Press, 1974.

Maes, John L. *Suffering: A Caregivers Guide.* Nashville, Tenn.: Abingdon Press, 1990.

Moore, Thomas. *Care of the Soul: A Guide for Cultivating Depth and Sacredness in Everyday Life.* New York: Harper-Collins, 1992.

———. *Soul Mates: Honoring Mysteries of Love and Relationships.* New York: HarperCollins, 1994.

Morgan, Nina. *Mother Teresa: Saint of the Poor.* Austin, Tex.: Steck Vaughn, 1998.

Muggeridge, Malcom. *Something Beautiful for God (Mother Teresa of Calcutta).* New York: Ballantine Books, 1978.

Otto, Rudolf. *The Idea of the Holy.* New York: Galaxy Books, 1958.

Palmer, Helen. *The Enneagram in Love and Work: Understanding Your Intimate and Business Relationships.* New York: HarperCollins, 1993.

Peers, E. Allison, ed. and trans. *St. John of the Cross: Ascent of Mt. Carmel.* Garden City, N.Y.: Image Books, 1958.

———. *St. Teresa of Avila: The Way of Perfection.* Garden City, N.Y.: Image Books, 1964.

Pope, Ira. *The Life and Work of Martin Luther King, Jr.* New York: Scholastic, 1968.

Progoff, Ira, trans. *The Cloud of Unknowing.* New York: Delta Books, 1957.

Ranier, Maria Rilke. Letter no. 13 in *Letters to a Young Poet.* Novato, Calif.: New World Library, 2000.

Underhill, Evelyn. *Practical Mysticism.* New York: E. P. Dutton, 1915.

Warner, Rex. *The Confessions of St. Augustine.* New York: Penguin Books, 1963.

Whittier, John Greenleaf. "Dear Lord and Father of Mankind," in *The Covenants Hymnal.* Chicago: Covenant Press, 1973.

Zukav, Gary. *The Seat of the Soul.* New York: Simon and Schuster, 1989.

Meditation

Benson, Herbert. *Beyond the Relaxation Response.* New York: Time Book, 1984.

———. *The Relaxation Response.* New York: William Murrow, 1975.

Bry, Adelaide. *Directing the Movies of Your Mind: Visualization for Health and Insight.* New York: Harper and Row, 1978.

Cohen, Alan. *Setting the Scene: Creative Visualization for Healing.* South Kortright, N.Y.: Eden, 1982.

Cooke, Grace. *Meditation.* Hampshire, Eng.: Eagle Publishing Trust, 1955.

Davis, Roy Eugene. *An Easy Guide to Meditation.* Lakemont, Ga.: CSH Press, 1978.

Easwaran, Eknath. *Meditation—Commonsense Directions for an Uncommon Life.* Petaluma, Calif.: Nilgiri Press, 1978.

Fischer, Kathleen. *The Inner Rainbow: The Imagination in Christian Life.* Ramsey, N.J.: Paulist Press, 1983.

Gendlin, Eugene T. *Focusing.* New York: Bantam Books, 1981.

Goleman, Daniel. *The Meditative Mind: The Varieties of Meditative Experience.* Los Angeles: Jeremy Tarcher, 1988.

Kelsey, Morton T. *The Other Side of Silence—A Guide to Christian Meditations.* New York: Paulist Press, 1976.

Le Shan, Lawrence. *How to Meditate: A Guide to Self Discovery.* Boston: Little Brown, 1974.

MacDonald-Bayne, Murdo. *How to Relax and Revitalise Yourself.* London: L. N. Fowler, 1952.

Meserve, Harry C. *The Practical Meditator.* New York: Human Services Press, 1981.

Moffat, Doris. *Christian Meditation the Better Way.* Chappaqua, N.Y.: Christian Herald Books, 1979.

Oliver, Fay Conlee. *Christian Growth Through Meditation.* Valley Forge, Pa.: Judson Press, 1976.

Progoff, Ira. *The Star/Cross—A Cycle of Process Meditation.* New York: Dialogue House Library, 1971.

——. *The Well and the Cathedral–A Cycle of Process Meditation.* New York: Dialogue House Library, 1971.
——. *The White Robed Monk–A Cycle of Process Meditation.* New York: Dialogue House Library, 1972.
Rajneesh, Bhagwan Shree. *Meditation: The Art of Ecstasy.* New York: Harper and Row, 1976.
Samuels, Mike and Nancy. *Seeing with the Mind's Eye: The History, Techniques and Uses of Visualization.* New York: Random House, 1975.
Sechrist, Elsie. *Meditation: Gateway to Light.* Virginia Beach, Va.: A.R.E. Press, 1972.
Stearn, Jess. *The Power of Alpha Thinking.* New York: American Library, 1976.
Troeger, Thomas H. *Meditation: Escape to Reality.* Philadelphia: Westminister Press, 1977.
Vaughan, Frances E. *Awakening Intuition.* New York: Anchor-Doubleday, 1979.

Healing

Achterberg, Jeanne. *Imagery in Healing.* Boston: Shambhala, 1985.
Althouse, Lawrence W. *Rediscovering the Gift of Healing.* Nashville, Tenn.: Abingdon Press, 1977.
Barasch, Marc Ian. *The Healing Path–A Soul Approach to Illness.* New York: G. P. Putnam's Sons, 1993.
Beard, Rebecca. *Everyman's Search.* Eversham, Eng.: Arthur James, 1951.
Beck, Mark. *The Theory and Practice of Therapeutic Massage.* New York: Milady, 1988.
Campbell, Don. The *Mozart Effect.* New York: Avon Books, 1997.
Clark, Glenn. *How to Find Health Through Prayer.* New York: Harper and Brothers, 1940.
Cooke, Ivan. *Healing by the Spirit.* Hampshire, England: White Eagle Publishing Trust, 1955.
Cousins, Norman. *The Healing Heart.* New York: Norton, 1983.
Daily, Starr. *Recovery.* St. Paul, Minn.: MacAlister Peak, 1975.
Dossey, Larry, M.D. *Healing Words: The Power of Prayer and the Practice of Medicine.* San Francisco: HarperSanFrancisco, 1993.
Erikson, Erik H. *Childhood and Society.* 2d Edition. New York: W. W. Norton, 1963.
Frazier, Claude A. *Faith Healing: Finger of God or Scientific Curiosity?* New York: Thomas A. Nelson, 1973.
Goldner, Diane. *Infinite Grace: Where the Worlds of Science and Spiritual Healing Meet.* Charlottesville, Va.: Hampton Roads, 1999.
Goldsmith, Joel S. *The Art of Spiritual Healing.* New York: Harper and Row, 1959.

Goodrich, Joyce. "Healing and Meditation, Healing as a Unitive Experience." *CTRP (Consciousness Training and Research Project) Newsletter* 17, no. 1 (May 1993).

Goodwin, Jan. "Amazing Grace." *Family Circle* (14 November 2000).

Hammerschlag, Carl A. *The Dancing Healers: A Doctor's Journey of Healing with Native Americans.* New York: Harper and Row, 1988.

Hannah, Barbara. *Active Imagination.* Boston, Mass.: Siego Press, 1981.

Houston, Jean. *The Search for the Beloved.* Los Angeles: Jeremy P. Tarcher, 1987.

Jackson, Edgar N. *The Role of Faith in the Process of Healing.* Minneapolis: Winston Press, 1981.

Jafolla, Richard. *Soul Surgery: The Ultimate Self-Healing.* Marina Del Rey, Calif.: Devoss, 1982.

Jourard, Sydney M. *The Transparent Self.* New York: D. Van Nostrand, 1964.

Kelsey, Morton T. *Healing and Christianity: Ancient Thought and Modern Times.* New York: Harper and Row, 1973.

Krieger, Dolores. *The Therapeutic Touch.* Englewood Cliffs, N.J.: Prentice-Hall, 1979.

Lester, Reginald M. *Towards the Hereafter with a Special Inquiry into Spiritual Healing.* New York: Citadel Press, 1957.

MacNutt, Francis. *The Prayer that Heals.* Notre Dame, Ind.: Ave Maria Press, 1981.

Major, Ralph H. *Faiths that Healed.* New York: Appleton Century, 1940.

Martin, Bernard. *The Healing Ministry in the Church.* Richmond, Va.: John Knox Press, 1960.

Martin, George. *Healing: Reflections on the Gospel.* Ann Harbor, Mich.: Servant Books, 1977.

Miner, Malcolm H. *Healing Is for Real.* New York: Morehouse-Barlow, 1972.

Neev, Elan Z. *Wholistic Healing.* Beverly Hills, Calif.: Ageless Books, 1977.

Oken, Donald. *Stress: Our Friend or Foe? Blueprint for Health.* Chicago: Blue Cross Association, Editorial Office, 1974.

Olshan, Neal. *Power over Your Pain without Drugs.* New York: Rawson Wade, 1983.

Ornish, Dean. *Love and Survival: The Scientific Basis for the Healing Power of Intimacy.* New York: Harper Collins, 1998.

Oursler, Will. *The Healing Power of Faith.* New York: Hawthorn Books, 1957.

Oyle, Irving. *The Healing Mind—You Can Cure Yourself without Drugs.* Millbrae, Calif.: Celestial Arts, 1975.

Pera, Gina. "Stress and Health." *The Christian Home* (Dec.–Feb. 1981–82).

Price, Reynolds. *A Whole New Life.* New York: Maxwell MacMillan, 1994.

Samuels, Mike and Nancy. *Seeing with the Mind's Eye.* New York: Random House, 1975.

Sanford, Agnes. *The Healing Light*. Plainfield, N.J.: Manchester Park, 1972.

Sanford, John A. *Healing Body and Soul: The Meaning of Illness in the New Testament and in Psychotherapy*. Louisville, Ky.: John Knox Press, 1992.

Sherwood, Keith. *The Art of Spiritual Healing: A Practical Guide to Healing Power*. St.Paul, Minn.: Llewellyn, 1985.

Weatherhead, Leslie D. *Psychology, Religion and Healing*. Nashville, Tenn.: Abingdon Press, 1952.

Dying and Death

Agee, James. *A Death in the Family*. New York: McDowell Obolensky, 1957.

Albom, Mitch. *Tuesdays with Morrie*. New York: Doubleday, 1997.

Berger, Arthur. *Perspectives on Death and Dying*. Philadelphia: Charles Press, 1989.

Bremyer, Jane. *Crossing*. Lindsburg, Kans.: Barbo-Carlson Enterprises, 2000.

Callanan, Maggie, and Patricia Kelley. *Final Gifts*. New York: Bantam Books, 1993.

Dempsey, David. *The Way We Die: An Investigation of Death and Dying in America Today*. New York: McGraw-Hill, 1977.

Donnelley, Nina Herrmann. *Go Out in Joy*. Atlanta: John Knox Press, 1977.

Fish, Mary Catherine. "Letting Go," *Readers Digest* (May 1999).

Foos-Graber, Anya. *Deathing: An Intelligent Alternative for the Final Moments of Life*. York Beach, Me.: Nicolas-Hays, 1989.

Frankl, Victor E. *The Doctor and the Soul*. New York: Alfred A. Knopf, 1968.

Keleman, Stanley. *Living Your Dying*. Berkeley, Calif.: Center Press, 1974.

Kübler-Ross, Elisabeth. *Death—The Final Stage of Growth*. Englewood Cliffs, N.J.: Prentice-Hall, Inc., 1975.

———. *On Death and Dying*. New York: Macmillan, 1969.

———. *To Live Until We Say Goodbye*. With photographs by Mal Warshaw. New York: Prentice-Hall, 1978.

Lepp, Ignace. *Death and Its Mysteries*. New York: Macmillan, 1968.

Levine, Stephen. *Meetings at the Edge*. Garden City, N.Y.: Doubleday, 1984.

———. *A Year to Live*. New York: Bell Tower, 1997.

Nouwen, Henri. *Our Greatest Gift: A Meditation on Dying and Caring*. San Francisco: HarperCollins, 1994.

Pattison, E. Mansell. *The Experience of Dying*. Englewood Cliffs, N.J.: Prentice-Hall, 1977.

Pelgrin, Mark. *And a Time to Die.* Angel Island Publications, 1977.

Quezada, Anolpho. *Goodbye, My Son, Hello.* St. Meinard, Ind.: Abbey Press, 1985.

Shneidman, Edwin. *Voices of Death.* New York: Bantam Books, 1982.

Ufema, Joy. *Brief Companions.* Fawn Grove, Pa.: Mulligan, 1984.

Wertenbaker, Lael. *Death of a Man.* Boston, Mass.: Beacon Press, 1974.

Loss and Grief

Bloom-Feshbach, Jonathan and Sally. *The Psychology of Separation and Loss.* San Francisco: Jossey-Bass, 1987.

Challoner, H. K. *The Path of Healing: Finding Your Soul's Potential.* Wheaton, Ill.: Theosophical Publishing House, 1990.

Chesser, Barbara Russell. *Because You Care: Practical Ideas for Helping Those Who Grieve.* Waco, Tex.: Word Books, 1987.

Childs-Gowell, Elaine. *Good Grief Rituals: Tools for Healing.* Barrytown, N.Y.: Station Hill Press, 1992.

Davidson, Glen. *Understanding Mourning.* Minneapolis: Augsburg Press, 1984.

Deits, Bob. *Life After Loss.* Tucson, Ariz.: Fisher Books, 1988.

Droege, Thomas A. *Guided Grief Imagery: A Resource for Grief Ministry and Death Education.* New York: Paulist Press, 1987.

Erdahl, Lowell. *The Lonely House: Strength for Times of Loss.* Lima, Ohio: CSS, 1989.

Jackson, Edgar N., *You and Your Grief.* New York: Hawthorne Books, 1962.

James, John W., and Frank Cherry. *The Grief Recovery Handbook: A Step-By-Step Program for Moving Beyond Loss.* New York: Harper and Row, 1988.

Koers, Shirley. *The Eyes Are Sunlight: A Journey Through Grief.* Notre Dame, Ind.: Ave Maria Press, 1986.

Krauss, Pesach. *Why Me? Coping with Grief, Loss and Change.* New York: Bantam Books, 1988.

Kreeft, Peter. *Love Is Stronger than Death.* San Francisco: Harper and Row, 1979.

Manning, Doug. *Don't Take My Grief Away from Me: How to Walk Through Grief and Learn to Live Again.* Hereford, Tex.: In-Sight Books, 1979.

Nelson, Harold R. *Understanding and Handling Our Grief.* Chicago: Covenant Press, 1970.

O'Connor, Nancy. *Letting Go with Love: The Grieving Process.* Apache Junction, Ariz.: La Mariposa Press, 1984.

Price, Eugenia. *Getting Through the Night: Finding Your Way After the Loss of a Loved One.* New York: Ballantine Books, 1982.

Raphael, Beverley. *The Anatomy of Bereavement.* New York: Basic Books, 1983.

Smith, Joanne, and Judy Biggs. *How to Say Goodbye: Working Through Personal Grief.* Lynnwood, Wash.: Aglow Publications, 1990.

Tatelbaum, Judy. *The Courage to Grieve: Creative Living, Recovery and Growth Through Grief.* New York: Harper and Row, 1990.

Westberg, Granger. *Good Grief.* Philadelphia: Fortress Press, 1962.

Worden, J. William. *Grief Counseling and Grief Therapy.* New York: Springer, 1982.

Zanca, Kenneth J. *Mourning: The Healing Journey.* Locust Valley, N.Y.: Living Flame Press, 1980.

Afterlife

Addison, J. T. *Life Beyond Death in the Beliefs of Mankind.* New York: Houghton Mifflin, 1932.

Badham, Paul. *Christian Beliefs about Life After Death.* New York: Barnes and Noble Books, 1977.

Barrett, William. *Death–bed Visions.* London, England: Methuen, 1926.

Becker, Ernest. *The Denial of Death.* Chicago: Free Press, 1973.

Colton, Ann Ree. *Men in White Apparel.* Glendale, Calif.: Arc Publishing, 1961.

Ettinger, Robert C. *The Prospect of Immortality.* Garden City, N.Y.: Doubleday, 1964.

Fortman, Edmund J. *Everlasting Life After Death.* New York: Albra House, 1977.

Greeley, Andrew M. *Death and Beyond.* Chicago: Thomas More Press, 1976.

Guggenheim, Bill and Judy. *Hello from Heaven.* New York: Bantam Books, 1996.

Hick, John H. *Death and Eternal Life.* New York: Harper and Row, 1977.

Holzer, Hans. *Beyond This Life.* New York: Pinnacle Books, 1977.

Kelsey, Morton. *Afterlife: The Other Side of Dying.* New York: Crossroad, 1979.

Kübler-Ross, Elisabeth. *On Life After Death.* Berkley, Calif.: Celestial Arts, 1991.

MacGregor, Geddes. *Reincarnation in Christianity.* Wheaton, Ill.: Theosphical Publishing House, 1978.

Monroe, Robert A. *Journeys Out of the Body.* Garden City, N.Y.: Doubleday, 1971.

Myers, Frederick W. *Human Personality and Its Survival of Bodily Death.* New York: Amro Press, 1975.

Myers, John, compiler. *Voices from the Edge of Eternity.* Old Tappan, N.J.: Fleming H. Revell, 1971.

Osis, Karlis, and Erlendur Haraldsson. *At the Hour of Death.* New York: Avon Books, 1971.

Rawlings, Maurice. *Beyond Death's Door*. Nashville, Tenn.: Thomas Nelson, 1978.

Swedenborg, Emanuel. *Heaven and Its Wonders and Hell: From Things Heard and Seen*. New York: American Swedenborg Printing and Publishing Society, 1925.

Toynbee, Arnold. *Life After Death*. New York: McGraw-Hill, 1976.

Weldon, John, and Zola Levitt. *Is There Life After Death?* Irvine, Calif.: Harvest House Publications, 1977.

The Near-Death Experience

Atwater, P. H. M. *Beyond the Light*. New York: Birth Lane Press, 1994.

Blackmore, Susan. *Dying to Live*. Buffalo, N.Y.: Prometheus Books, 1993.

Brinkley, Dannion. *At Peace in the Light*. New York: Harper-Collins, 1995.

Cox-Chapman, Mally. *The Case for Heaven*. New York: G. P. Putnam and Sons, 1995.

Cressy, Judith. *The Near-Death Experience: Mysticism or Madness?* Hanover, Mass.: Christopher Publishing House, 1994.

Eadie, Betty. *Embraced by the Light*. Placerville, Calif.: Gold Leaf Press, 1992.

Fenimore, Angie. *Beyond the Darkness*. New York: Bantam Books, 1995.

Flynn, Charles P. *After the Beyond*. Englewood-Cliffs, N.J.: Prentice Hall, 1986.

Moody, Raymond, Jr. *Life After Life*. New York: Bantam Books, 1976.

———. *Reflections on Life after Life*. Covington, Ga.: Mocking Bird Books, 1977.

Rhodes, Leon. *Tunnel to Eternity: Swedenborgians Look Beyond the Near-Death Experience*. Byrn Athyn, Pa.: L.S. Rhodes,1996.

Ring, Kenneth. *Heading Toward Omega*. New York: Quill, 1985.

———. *Life at Death*. New York: Coward, McCann and Geoghegan, 1980.

Ring, Kenneth, and Sharon Cooper. *Mindsight*. Palo Alto, Calif.: William James Consciousness Studies at the Institute of Transpersonal Psychology, 1999

———. "Near-death and out of body experiences in the blind. A study of apparent eyeless vision." *Journal of Near-Death Studies* (Winter 1997).

Ring, Kenneth, and Evelyn Valarino. *Lessons from the Light*. New York: Insight Books, 1998.

Ritchie, George. *My Life After Dying*. Norfolk, Va.: Hampton Roads, 1991.

———. *Return from Tomorrow*. Grand Rapids, Mich.: Fleming H. Revell, 1988.

Sabom, Michael B. *Recollections of Death*. New York: Harper and Row, 1982.

Storm, Howard R. *My Descent into Death and the Message of Love which Brought Me Back*. London: Clairview Books, 2000.

Sutherland, Cherie. *Reborn in the Light*. New York: Bantam, 1995.

Tart, Charles. *Open Mind, Discriminating Mind*. New York: Harper and Row, 1987.

Vincent, Ken R. *Visions of God: From the Near-Death Experience*. Burdestt, N.Y.: Larson, 1994.

Zaleski, Carol. *The Life of the World to Come: Near-Death Experiences and Christian Hope*. New York: Oxford Press, 1996.

———. *Otherworld Journeys: Account of Near-Death Experiences in Medieval and Modern Times*. New York: Oxford Press, 1987.